Hea
From
Infidelity

A Survival Guide for Happy Couples. Let's Save a Contemporary Marriage From the Main Issue of Our Generation: The Divorce!

MELODY ROMIG

Text Copyright © [Melody Romig]

Legal & Disclaimer

Table of Contents

Introduction

As devastating as it sounds, infidelity has become more rampant in modern society than in the past. For many people, infidelity is a cut and dry act—an engagement in sexual activity of any kind with a different person apart from your partner, while for others, cheating can mean several physical activities that a partner engages in, which ought to be reserved exclusively for couples. No one understands for sure how common infidelity occurs. While the landscape of infidelity is changing, the world has remained fixed in the belief that the affairs result from the things that are wrong with the marriage. But make no mistake; many people in relationships or marriages always want to stay together even after their partners have strayed, despite the psychological and emotional trauma that is involved in the act. Also, more than 70 percent of couples choose to forgive and rebuild their relationships once infidelity has occurred, although they never know how. Understanding the causes of infidelity and its impact is the first step toward learning how to effectively heal from infidelity.

Studies have repeatedly highlighted the daunting effects of infidelity. A person who is cheated on will always lose his or her self-esteem, always trying to take the blame for the cheating. "Was I not enough?" or "What did I do wrong to push my partner to cheat?" are common questions that victims of infidelity ask. Infidelity also results in the loss of trust in the cheating partner. A victim of an affair will lose trust in his or her partner. Even after a relationship ends, they would still have trust issues, which may not only affect their relationships but also their environment at work or school. Additionally, infidelity results in emotional instability and a roller coaster of emotions. Cheating may make the victimized partner blame themselves and have an emotional imbalance, which may affect their daily productivity.

To that end, this book provides an in-depth overview of infidelity, including the causes and effects and how to heal from infidelity. It provides an understanding of the concept of infidelity by first providing a case study of a couple who have dealt with infidelity and how they were able to solve it. The book then provides a definition of the concept, highlighting that there is no clear-cut definition. Furthermore, examples of physical scenarios that may be considered avenues of betrayal have been covered. The book addresses the three types of infidelity, including emotional, physical, and commemorative infidelity. This information will enable you to understand how infidelity occurs and the meaning as understood by different people.

This book will also cover the symptoms and ways to prevent infidelity. Some of the common symptoms of infidelity before and after marriage including improvement in the appearance of your partner, a partner becoming secretive when it comes to their mobile devices, a partner no longer having time for the other person, and a change of different sex patterns in the relationship. Furthermore, when a partner, all of sudden, becomes hostile to the partner, changes his or her schedule and routines, or your lover's friends become uncomfortable around you, it could mean that your partner is unfaithful. By understanding these symptoms, as well as the causes of infidelity, you will be able to prevent your relationship from facing infidelity cases. Some of the measures to take to avoid cheating have been highlighted, including avoiding being with someone of the opposite sex, not drinking alcohol with the opposite sex, supporting your relationship, weighing the consequences of infidelity before trying it, and maintaining moral standards.

By reading this book, you will understand that the decision of a partner to cheat is never your fault, and although there have been several issues in the relationship, you never made a choice to betray your partner. It is critical to understand that it is never about you, but the cheating partner who had a lot of deficiencies that he or she could not deal with amicably. Your partner and you will be very grateful that you prevent or deal with infidelity in a proper manner, and you will be able to trust each other once more. You will also develop the critical skills of managing a relationship after an incident of infidelity. Apart from managing your anger, this book will discuss ways of managing resentment and restoring trust in a cheating partner.

Many individuals are also trapped in abusive marriages because of the children. Some are abused emotionally, while others physically as a result of infidelity. It is important to understand that most people who hurt the most in such marriages are the children. You should not lose hope! Everyone has an opportunity to be happy, and by leaving an unhappy marriage, one is able to get an opportunity to love again. This book will provide you with the necessary information on when to decide to quit and how to move on after separating from a cheating partner. Some of the important steps to take when making the decision of separation should include consulting a lawyer, deciding on whether you want the separation, coming up with a plan, canceling all your joint credit cards, closing your joint accounts, and documenting all your financial information to avoid legal repercussions that may be associated with separation.

The information covered in this book is very important as it can change your life and that of your partner. For this book to work for you, it is vital that you encompass all the advice and techniques you have read herein. It may not be in the order that they are listed in this book, but you may consider using all of them for maximum benefits. You are now aware of what you need to do to overcome infidelity, regardless of the cause. Next thing you would want to do is put in a request for what you want. By reading this book until the end, you will get the opportunity to start over a relationship that is full of trust and empathy. These are all necessary for emotional fulfillment.

Chapter 1:
What Is Infidelity?

When one of my best friends, Kelly, visited me on a Sunday evening, she could not hide her torment. She helplessly sat on the dining table, fidgeting her hands and feet. I looked at her for a moment, and tears began rolling down her cheeks.

"I think Jayden is cheating on me," she said.

I had suspected that Kelly had a serious issue. Since our college years, I have never seen her this angry. She has always been a beautiful, calm girl who is never offended by issues. However, recently, I realized she was a bit distant from her boyfriend, Jayden, of over 6 years. While hanging out, she would avoid his calls, though I never understood the reason since she avoided the topic repeatedly.

"Why would you accuse him of doing that? Please talk to me," I responded.

Kelly explained to me that, in recent weeks, Jayden has been receiving calls from different women and would also ignore them when they are together. He would also constantly chat until late at night after she had gone to bed. When Kelly confronted him about it, he got mad and accused Kelly of being insecure and making a big deal out of nothing. This made Kelly stop talking to him and avoid taking his calls. Two days ago, while in his house, she checked his phone and found that he was flirting with two different women, sharing sexual messages with both of them. They confronted each other, and she left him.

Defining Infidelity

Normally, before two people begin engaging in an affair or getting married, there is always a need to set the parameters of the relationship. At some point in a relationship, people tend to ask, "Are we exclusively dating each other?" If the answer to this question is yes, then the process of excluding others from the relationship and developing trust begins. Once individuals decide to form such a committed relationship, however, few couples always open up the discussion of "infidelity." Thus, there is never a particular definition of infidelity that can fit every unfaithful situation.

When a person accuses the partner of cheating, a long string of explanations and explorations begin. In case there is solid proof, such as footage showing engagement in sexual activity, then there is never an opportunity for interpretation. However, more than 90 % of infidelity cases do not have such proof of adultery. In fact, many people are like Kelly, where the issue of cheating is only based on hints rather than facts. If relationship and commitment rules have only been broken through spirit, do we still refer to it as infidelity? That depends on how every relationship understands infidelity.

According to the Oxford Dictionary, 'infidelity' refers to adultery or 'marital disloyalty.' The dictionary defines adultery as the engagement of a married person in sexual relations with a different party other than the partner. This means that infidelity can only take place after marriage. It is, however, complex than that since individuals or couples may choose to be in a long-term, committed relationship that requires everyone to be faithful to the other.

Infidelity, which can also be referred to as cheating or straying or adultery when married, is an act of being unfaithful to your spouse or other sexual partners. This constitutes a violation of a partners' contract, either assumed or stated, regarding sexual and emotional exclusivity.

Physical Understanding of Infidelity

There are several physical aspects of infidelity, which influences the way affairs might be defined. Consider the following physical cases committed by a person who is committed in a relationship:

- Engaging in oral sex with another person
- Engaging in manual sex with another person apart from the partner
- Touching another person's genitals without penetration
- Kissing another person
- Touching himself or herself (or engaging in other sexual acts) without partner's knowledge

Consider the examples above; it may seem pretty obvious that they result in infidelity. But one may ask, "What if these activities are done with a prostitute during a single business trip?" Would it still be referred to as an affair? What if a partner received a "relief massage" from a masseuse who was performing manual sex—would the man be considered to have cheated on the wife?

You may find that the above scenarios are examples of infidelity. However, it does not mean that the person with whom you are committed or married defines infidelity in the same way.

Physical contact may also be interpreted depending on whether they are overtly sexual or non-sexual acts. Consider the following nonsexual physical contacts existing between a married person and one who is not married:

- Holding each other's hands
- Hugging each other
- Sitting on the other person's lap
- Allowing legs to touch each other
- Playfully punching another person while teasing
- Lingering fingers on each other while passing objects to one another

Several couples experience marital fissures over the above events. For many, any physical or suggestive contact with the opposite sex or an attractive person who is not a partner could be interpreted as infidelity.

Let us consider the story of Kelly and Jayden. After a few weeks of the break-up, they both decided to confront the issue. Jayden revealed that he did not go any further than flirting with the two girls. He admitted having engaged in sexual conversations with the two coworkers, who were both juniors of Kelly, discussing issues pertaining to marriage and relationships. He had also visited both of them on several occasions, but they never did anything that is sexually related. According to him, they only held hands passionately and would touch each other's legs with no sexual intention.

At this point in the case, Kelly was very sure that Jayden had slept with both women. She could not believe that he could have gotten so close to those women without making any sexual advances. It is interesting to note that it was very clear in Jayden's mind that although he would have wished to go further with the two women, he decided not to proceed with any sexual advances because he was committed to Kelly. He believed that he avoided infidelity. However, in Kelly's thoughts there was infidelity because there was some form of physical and emotional touch with other women.

To solve the issue, the couple decided to come up with the guidelines of their relationship to avoid any misunderstanding. They talked about the limited interactions with other people that would result in misinterpretation. By knowing what each of them understood by appropriate and inappropriate behaviors, they promised to restrict their social interactions to those permissible by the other.

Types of Infidelity

There are different types of infidelity that one may face while in a relationship. Understanding each one of them is very important not to fall prey to any of them. It is also important to know the types of infidelity so that you can continue to nourish and work on your own relationship.

There are three major types of infidelity: emotional, physical, and commemorative infidelity. These categories help in understanding the reasons that individuals engage in any form of infidelity and the actions involved in the type of infidelity.

Emotional Infidelity

Emotional infidelity refers to an affair that occurs when a partner in a relationship becomes emotionally entangled to someone else other than the partner. When committing emotional infidelity, your partner may be spending more time communicating with someone else about important or personal things to enjoy making jokes with them. It may also involve the sharing of issues, life goals, and problems with another person that is not your spouse; this may take away your attention from your existing relationship.

An important aspect of emotional infidelity is object affair, in which a partner begins to pursue a particular interest outside the relationship that may result in an obsession, where the interest causes negligence. It is usually encouraged that individuals have a healthy balance between their relationships and outside interests.

A cyber affair is also a form of emotional infidelity, although it occurs entirely online. It involves the act of video calling, chatting, texting, and sexting. Performing these activities with a person other than your partner is an indication of infidelity.

Physical Infidelity

Physical infidelity refers to the act of engaging in sexual intercourse or sexual relations away from one's relationship. Examples of physical infidelity is a one-night-stand or sleeping with a prostitute. Having sexual exclusivity or monogamy is as important as having a healthy sex life.

A common form of physical infidelity is opportunistic infidelity, which generally occurs when one partner loves the other spouse but succumbs to the opportunity to engage in sexual activity with another person. Alcohol and drug use are always involved in this form of infidelity, thereby inhibiting one's ability to stay faithful.

Commemorative Infidelity

This type of infidelity occurs when a partner in a relationship is not getting enough sexual or physical attention that they desire. In many cases, the act of cheating is always justified by the person seeking what they are unable to receive from the relationship. Such relationships always lack any emotional attachment, which allows the person to express their desires elsewhere.

6 Causes of Infidelity

What makes anyone want to cheat on their marriage or relationship? This is a question you must be asking yourself. If you have been a victim of infidelity, then you have asked yourself various questions. There are many consequences that come with adultery, and you will want to know why your partner decided to cheat. There are many reasons associated with the many cases of infidelity and cheating. Any case of adultery varies and has a different purpose. When you find out the status of your partner cheating, then it will bring a lot of confusion to you. This can make you either move on or decide to have a divorce. When you understand the causes of infidelity, it becomes the first step in enhancing your relationship after being in an affair. This is because you will be able to identify the source of the issue and try to get a solution. You should be able to understand why people cheat. Below are the causes of infidelity.

When You Feel the Relationship Is One-Sided

One most prominent problem that couples face before infidelity is the presence of an imbalance in the relationship. One-sided relationships can be in different forms where one spouse will feel as if they are unappreciated, or one partner feels they have a lot of financial strains than the other, among others. As long as you think you have more weight in a relationship than your partner, then that is one-sided. With so much pressure of contact, you may want to seek relief from another relation.

Lack of Communication

For a successful relationship to take place, communication is part of the pillars for a stable relationship. You have to create time for your partner and always listen to them because if you do not, then you will have difficulties in solving issues in your marriage. Lack of communication is one feature among people who cheat. They will not be able to share anything with their spouses, thus making them seek some attention elsewhere, leading to cheating. When you are struggling to solve your issues in a relationship, it is high time you get some help from a marriage counselor.

Lack of Enough Sex

Many people are cheating because they do not get enough sex at home. This does not affect men only but everyone in a relationship. Either a man or woman can decide to cheat due to a lack of suitable sexual activities. A study has shown that 52 % of people who do not get satisfied with their sex lives are usually tempted to get their desires fulfilled with people they are attracted to. Anyone who does not get a good sex life is three times likely to cheat in the relationships, unlike those who are satisfied. The study also tells us that 71 % of men who cheated did it due to sexual boredom compared to only 49 % of women.

Lousy sex life will bring some problems in your relationship. You may be worried about infidelity because of your sex life; thus, you should try sex therapy. You and your partner will be forced to work with a therapist to help enhance your intimacy and marital status. You will have new techniques on how to be with your spouse, and to correct the past issues with your relationship that had affected your sex life.

Unfulfilled Sex Drive

There is this excuse that you have heard before, like "my sex drive is high for one partner to help me out or handle it." Men will mostly say this statement, and women also have high sex drives, too. There can be problems with sexual fulfillment in your relationship and correcting those problems can help you keep off infidelity together. You can have some active sex life, but still, your partner will cheat on you, and this will be due to some personal difficulties that one needs to report. You should not have an excuse to cheat on your spouse due to high sex drive; 46 % of men and 19 % of women who cheated have been cited for cheating because of this. You can have some feeling that your sex life is not fully meeting your wants. With such problems, you are advised to try to seek help from a counselor and talk about how you will satisfy your desires.

Revenge for Past Activities

You may not want to believe it, but many couples decide to cheat because they were cheated on before. There are situations where the non-cheater finds it is difficult to forgive the person who cheated; thus, they may want to cheat for revenge. This is a harrowing cycle that will bring about more pain than comfort, and this will cause infidelity. You can work with your spouse when you think you are at risk of cheating, or you want to improve your relationship by visiting a counselor who can assist you to go through the problem and move on peacefully.

Boredom

When you are bored, you can be tempted to have an affair. A lot of you have been going through routines, which include the same methods in the bedroom. You have to get some activities that will always keep your relationship fresh. A lot of divorce cases can be avoided when people create time for each other and become committed to verbal communication, as well as physical communication, which might just bring some excitement. Many people will look for excitement to avoid becoming bored, and this can be seen when they get to other relationships, start using drugs, or get engaged to different people.

Infidelity, most of the time, will violate an agreement between two people; this will bring a negative attitude toward relationships. Friendship may bring some connection and will develop with time, thus bringing an intimate relationship. Platonic friendship will turn to an affair when it is emotionally intimate and has some privacy involved.

Disconnection from your partner may lead to infidelity. Many people complain of being unappreciated or loved, thus leading them to cheat on their spouses. Most of these feelings and secrets will lead to doing something that is not right, which may bring regret later on in the relationship.

Factors Predisposing a Partner to Infidelity

Studies have shown that over 40 % of married people have cheated at least once in the entire duration of their marriage.

Several factors predispose people to cheat. Affairs are usually triggered by risk factors, such as poor boundaries, opportunities presenting itself in social media, childhood issues, and infidelity disorders.

Some of the other risk factors leading to infidelity are frustrations in marriage, poor communication between couples, and the desire to get revenge or to hurt the other partner. The following are some of the risk factors that can make you predisposed to infidelity.

Lack of Attention from the Partner

Men tend to cheat more than women. This is because a man is likely to seek attention and sex more than a woman; therefore, when a man is not sexually satisfied by a spouse who consistently rejects their sexual advances, they tend to take that rejection seriously. To a man, sexual rejection may mean their spouses do not love them enough. This feeling of insecurity is what usually drives most men to cheat.

On the other hand, a woman cheats to fill an emotional void. Whenever a woman feels a form of disconnect from her partner, they tend to cheat. A woman wishes to be loved, desired, and cherished at all times by their spouses. When this fails to happen, they often feel they are not appreciated enough or that they are ignored. They will then seek intimacy from outside partners.

Addictions

Addiction to a substance, such as drugs and alcohol, and gambling are some of the other risk factors that can trigger infidelity. When you consume too much alcohol, your inhibitions are significantly reduced, and you are easily tempted to cross the line and cheat.

It is also common for some partners to use the cover of alcohol to gain the courage to cheat. Alcohol lowers your judgment and often makes you feel relaxed and carefree. Such individuals often blame alcohol for their cheating ways.

Previous History of Cheating

It is a commonly held belief that once a person cheats on their partner, they are likely to cheat again whenever an opportunity presents itself. This can happen even in their next relationship. A study conducted in 2017 showed that people involved in infidelity before meeting new partners are three times more likely to cheat again on their new love.

Psychological Issues and Personality Disorders

People with psychological problems or some personality disorders are more likely to cheat. Studies have established that people with narcissist tendencies, for example, are more likely to cheat. Moreover, people with personality disorders, such as those suffering from an antisocial personality disorder, are also more prone to cheating. Narcissists are often self-centered and lack any sense of empathy; therefore, they most likely engage in cheating to boost their ego. They usually do not acknowledge the impact their actions will have on their partners.

Childhood Issues

Some unresolved childhood issues can drive one to cheat on their partner. If you experience a childhood traumatic experience that could be in the form of sexual, physical, or emotional abuse, then you are at a higher risk of cheating. Besides, if you were exposed to infidelity at a younger age, then you are more likely to cheat. Studies have shown that the children who were exposed to a cheating parent while growing up are three times more likely to cheat on their partners.

Sexual Addiction

Sexual addiction is often blamed for infidelity, cheating, and promiscuity. People who are sex addicts often engage in dangerous sexual acts without considering the negative consequences of their actions. Sex addicts are often more likely to cheat on their partners. A sex addict usually looks to get high through sex. Moreover, most sex addicts abuse drugs, further aggravating their problem because they tend to lose control when under the influence.

Unhappiness or Dissatisfaction in Marriage

When you are unhappy with your marriage or your partner, then are likely to cheat. Marriage usually involves a lot of work and input from both partners. When the couple fails to nurture their marriage mutually, then they will grow distant and apart. This may lead them to cheat. Besides, a union with no intimacy presents a high risk for the partners to cheat.

Looking for the Thrill

When one is jaded and is looking for some form of excitement or a thrill, they can easily be tempted to engage in an affair. This applies to both men and women, regardless of their age and race. Such people tend to look for a thrill of the chase and excitement often found in a new love. Such people take their affairs as a way of spicing up their boring marriages. When couples fail to understand the maturing of love in their marriage, they tend to look for new love elsewhere.

Opportunity

There are some couples who are driven to cheat simply because a good opportunity to do so presented itself. Such opportunities usually come in the form of prolonged absence of their partners from home because of traveling or if one partner is serving in a faraway military posting. This could also apply to couples in long-distance relationships.

When you know your spouse is absent for long, you may be tempted to cheat, knowing too well that you stand low risks of being found. Moreover, long absences by one partner often lead to loneliness and some form of resentment, which may drive one to easily cheat.

Suspicions of Cheating

Some partners rightly or wrongly suspect their spouses of cheating, but they lack substantial evidence to confirm their suspicions. Due to frustrations at finding the truth, such couples may easily be tempted to cheat out of curiosity. Their minds are often preoccupied with the actions of their spouses, which raises their suspicions. When your mind is overly preoccupied with the prospect of your partner cheating on you, and you are frustrated at finding out the truth, you may end up cheating to feel better.

Social Media and the Internet

Social media has made cheating much easier, especially emotional cheating. Social media has been blamed for so many affairs and divorces. You should be aware that emotional cheating is still considered a form of cheating, even if you have had no physical contact with the other person.

Chapter 2:

How to Prevent Infidelity

A lot of people will be able to put up with high levels of self-control. You can be in a situation where you want to be with one partner, and this will lead to soul-searching. Infidelity will make you arrive at a situation where you are not supposed to. You can resist cheating when you put yourself in such situations beforehand. Try avoiding giving your number to people you just met, or avoid meeting people you might be attracted to. On the other hand, you can do everything right, and your partner could still have some reasons to be tempted to cheat on you. You can be in a position where everything is going well in your life, but again, sometimes, you just can't miss the desire to have more.

We tend to have so many positive choices and actions when it comes to promoting monogamy, such as having a pledge with the partner, dedication to the relationship, and commitment to the partner. However, even with such, we still have affairs happening. Research says that 90% of humans have been reported to be in a situation of cheating on their partner, and others have engaged in infidelity in a way or another. Adultery is considered a worldwide problem. Unfaithfulness is a big monster, affecting so many relationships across more than 160 countries, and this is according to research. A lot of people would like to engage and maintain monogamy, but still, there is some attraction to infidelity that makes them unsuccessful in their efforts to be faithful. Some people are unsuccessful in maintaining monogamy, but when you have a purpose for the relationship, you will overcome the strength of attraction to other parties and improve self-control.

Prediction of Infidelity

There is a study that shows how heterosexual couples behave when they are attracted to other people. Married partners were tested if they can divert their attention away from attractive faces, and there were a fair number of individuals with unfavorable levels of infidelity, according to the results. The research was conducted on 233 newlywed partners, who were three years into the relationship. They were asked about the issue of cheating, and pictures of lovely individuals of the opposite sex were shown to them. To conduct the study, a machine was there to determine how long it took for them to look away. They were also supposed to rate the faces, and the outcome was compared to the result of single individuals who rated the same pictures.

Positive Intentions Are Still Futile

Many people are still struggling against infidelity, and many strategies promoting monogamy are still unable to prevent cheating. There was a study done by a researcher on heterosexual individuals on how they deal with outside temptation when in relationships and if they were pushed to go on with the affair. According to the results, almost three-quarters of the respondents tried to be friendly, humble, loving, and intimate to enhance their relationships to avoid threats of being lonely or being attracted to someone else. There are various reasons that men and women cheat. Understanding it will help prevent infidelity from ruining your relationship.

1. Persist on love and care

At times, the demonstrations were verbal in love and care. On some occasions, they were physical, and such increases their feelings toward each other, thus reducing any temptation to cheat. For you to improve fidelity in your relationship, you have to create a significant connection with your partner, be grateful to him or her and try to be physically loving.

2. Improve your physical appearance

When you improve your facial and physical appearance, you will be more successful in maintaining your lover's attention. Aside from this, you can go to the salon or spa, buy new clothes, and engage in exercises, among others. Most importantly, doing these things will help you feel better about yourself and make you more confident.

3. Make them feel special through gifts

Getting them some special, such as a gift or some sexual attention, may help keep your partner happy and faithful. This is similar to rewarding your partner for his or her loyal character. Doing this will make both of you happy. When you reward your partner, the chances of making them comfortable and faithful become high.

4. Maintain having sex

Men will maintain intimacy because sex connects them and keep the relationship. Women mostly want to feel loved before they engage in any sexual activities. For men, they will feel loved after having sex, and sex life is a very crucial thing to support a healthy marriage. You will find it hard to believe that a couple would tell a divorce lawyer that too much sex was the reason behind splitting. Healthy sex life between couples improves the union and prevents infidelity in most cases.

5. Have positive connections

Sex and time are not enough to keep your relationship on a faithful note; you have to spend quality time together. The need for quality time may vary for some people, and you have to cherish the moments when you can spend time with each other. When spending quality time, you can pick a date night each week, have some time away from the kids, or simply spend time with your partner on the couch, talking about your day. There might be so many things happening in your daily lives, but you must create some time for such connections with your partner regularly.

6. Keep no secrets

One of the things that can bring about infidelity is keeping secrets from your partner but divulging your marital issues to someone outside your marriage. You have to avoid any secrets between you and your partner, including the things about your family and friends. Your friends should be aware that you share everything with your partner.

7. Get an open-book life

A happy marriage is usually composed of partners whose individual lives are considered "open book." This means you avoid keeping secrets from your partner. It also means it is okay for each partner to access one's phone, email, calendars or schedule, and social media accounts simply because there is nothing to hide. Partners maintain this type of openness because they are confident toward each other, not because they do not trust their partner.

Cheating can have a significant impact on monogamous relationships. Most people enhance cynical and emotionally manipulative tactics to help or make their lovers faithful. Such behaviors may not work and could be unproductive. To make your partner loyal, you have to motivate them, and that will keep them from cheating on you. Just try to express love and care to them. And remember to employ the techniques discussed earlier.

Symptoms of Marital Infidelity

If you start asking yourself what makes your partner cheat, then there is a probability that you are going to be a victim of infidelity, or you are having problems in your relationship. The signs of cheating between a couple vary in each relationship, and some details about the partnership can quickly tell you that there is a void in the relationship that needs to be filled. If your instincts tell you that your partner is cheating, then there is a high probability that you are right. With that, you will be curious to know the truth and find an explanation for the changes in your partner's character and behavior.

Your partner can come home late, smelling another person's scent, and this can tell you there is something that is not right. But there are sure signs that your partner is cheating. Cheating in marriages also happens to good people who are in good marriages and relationships.

1. Their appearance improves

When your partner starts to eat healthier, that is most probably a reason that they are trying to impress someone. A guy can start being neat, wearing fashionable clothes, and putting on designer perfumes just to be appealing to another woman. You will notice that when they are around you, they do not put any effort into their appearance, but when going out, they look better.

2. They are secretive when it comes to their phone or computer

Those who cheat will use their phones and computers most of the time, and they will do anything to protect their contents as if it is everything in their life. You may notice that your partner has a password on their phone or computer, which was something that was not there before, and this is not a good sign. In addition, such partners may start deleting texts and clearing the history on their browsers daily, and this is not a good sign, too. Your guilty partner may hinder you from accessing their phones or computer; they may even carry them to the bathroom. This behavior is definitely suspicious.

When your partner refuses to let you access their phone and review it, there are some chances of cheating.

3. They have no time for you

When your partner is cheating on you, their time is always limited when it comes to you. They are always busy at work, and they are always in a business meeting after work. They are unable to answer your calls or reply to your texts. Most of them will come up with excuses, such as they were held up in meetings, or they were driving. They will come up with the most creative excuses that will justify why they are not answering the call, why they are late, or why they are cold toward you. With the thoughts of the ugly possibility of cheating, it can be dreadful when your partner is out for a trip, and you can't reach them, or they are working out "late."

4. You have different sex patterns in your relationship

When there is an increase or decrease in sexual activities with your partner, it can also be a sign of infidelity. A decrease in the frequency of sex may be a sign that your partner has focused on another person. At the same time, having more sex with you can be a sign that your partner is trying to cover up that there is a third party involved. You can also tell that there is some infidelity in your relationship when you have sex, but there is no emotional connection between the two of you. Your partner may start bringing new sex styles and activities to your bedroom life. You might enjoy the new styles, but it can also be a trick learned from cheating with a third party.

5. There is hostility toward a partner and relationship

Those people cheating in relationships will try to rationalize their character. They will want to put the responsibility or blame on the other partner. The partner who was betrayed may hear excuses, such as: "You are not the same person I met at first," "You are not active in the bedroom nowadays," "You do not appreciate the things that I am doing for you," or "You are never around; we do not see each other often anymore." These lines allow the cheating partner to justify why they slept with someone else, but only when the other partner found out about it.

6. There is a change of schedule

A partner who never worked late, suddenly, out of nowhere, started coming home late because of "work." This may be a lie. Your spouse has never been out on a business trip, but suddenly, they need to travel for work. This excuse becomes their free ticket to spend some time with someone else. Other than these, there are other "reasons" for not being around, which are excuses to hide or mask infidelity. These are punctured car tire, dead phone battery, traffic jams, and longer gym time. Cheating partners may also forget about their duty to pick up the kids from school; they might miss birthday parties, as well as other important events in the family.

7. Your partner's friends are uncomfortable being with you

Where there is infidelity in the relationship, it is possible that you are the last person to know about it; thus, his or her friends will feel uncomfortable meeting you. The cheater's closest friends might be the first people to know about it. And your friends will likely find out about it from your common friends, and that is the only time you will learn about the infidelity. If the friends of your cheater partner cannot avoid you, they will probably be too nice to you, but they will avoid talking to you about certain topics.

8. Your partner has extra spending

Another sign of infidelity is your partner's changing spending habits. There can be a huge decrease in your partner's bank account and investment account, or their credit card spending skyrockets, among others. This could be a sign of infidelity. You can ask your partner about the changes, and when you get some answers that are simply ridiculous and untrue, then there is the possibility that they are lying.

Infidelity has a lot of expenditures attached to it: hotel room bookings, expenditure on wine and other liquor, expensive gifts, countless dinner dates, and quick coffee meet-ups, among many others. These activities can be expensive, thus adding up very quickly, depending on how frequent they meet. When you come across huge cash withdrawals or goods that certainly were not from the usual places you go to, there is a high probability that your partner is cheating on you.

9. Emotional feelings are fading

After being in a relationship for some years, no relationship will be the same the way it started. You will try to get along with each other, gaining trust in each other. This is creating or enhancing emotional feelings. Emotional intimacy keeps you bonded to your partner after you have been engaged immediately. If your partner changes in character or is less vulnerable and friendly with you and does not want to be vulnerable, then it is highly likely that their focus has turned to an affair with another partner.

10. Your partner avoids questions when you ask about cheating

When your partner is cheating on you, they will always not want to talk about the topic of cheating, and you might find them tensing up whenever the subject is brought up, even casually, at a dinner with friends or another situation. Whenever you bring up this topic in your conversations with your partner, there are signs that they do not want to talk about it, or they try to avoid the story altogether. Your partner will do anything to avoid talking about it, or they may bring up another story to divert what you are thinking. In case you ask your partner face-to-face if they are cheating on you, you would get a vague answer, such as "If only you had trust in me." If that is the case, then you should be worried about your relationship, and there is probably something wrong. From the previous discussion, if your instinct tells you that your partner is cheating on you, then it is more likely true.

There are times when your partner gives you such signs but still be faithful in a relationship. The symptoms are indications of infidelity in a relationship, and something is wrong. You may not see it as cheating, but it is something that you and your partner should talk about. You should also know that your partner may not show such symptoms and still cheat on you. When you learn about your partner's infidelity, it does not mean that it is automatically the end of your relationship. Your partner has a lot of work to do to keep their trust in relationships to make things okay between the two of you, as well as enhance emotional and sexual understanding. When you confirm that your partner is, indeed, cheating on you, then you should not keep that information to yourself. You can be uneasy about facing your partner, so you are advised to talk to a close friend, religious leaders like a pastor, or a therapist. You are not advised to sit with these feelings inside you; thus, you are encouraged to get some support. You can also find out more about how to cope and recover after suffering unfaithfulness from your partner.

Understanding How Affairs Begin

How do affairs begin? The betrayed partner, after finding out that his or her partner has been seeing a third lover, would usually like to know how it happened. Despite the pain you may be feeling, you would still like to know the gruesome details of the affair, such as when it happened, how they met, how long has it been going on, or if the other person is married.

You can take the example of two people who met for a drink after a business meeting. There are some things you have to be keen about. Did their knees touch under the table? Did one person put their arms around the other person's waist? Did they lie about where they are going? Did they lie about who they are sending those text messages to?

Many cases of divorce took place because either one lover or both had issues with the relationship. Research has shown the various reasons that most people start affairs, and these are:

1. They crave for certain qualities in a partner

Most people fall in love with the fantasy of the other person. You may be falling in love with a particular image you cultivate in your mind and the person you have manufactured in your thoughts. The partner in the affair was previously just an imaginary person who possesses qualities that meet your desires. When the opportunity presents itself, you find a reason to cheat on your partner with this person, thinking that they are ideal for you.

2. There is a need for extra validation that another person can give

Everyone will want to be appreciated and recognized for how nice they look or smell. Everyone wants to be valued, too. Many people who are cheating will not be in love with the third party, but they feel the need for an external validation, which they get from that partner. Thus, they feel as if they are in love when the affair starts.

3. It has become an adventure to find a new romance

The thing with infidelity is that when you find a new romance that validates you, you will be attached to the good feelings you get and not a person you are with. The act of cheating will make you think that the new person is your better half, and they can be better, unlike the partner that you have currently. Imagine a person who started cheating on his or her partner and then cheat on this other person with another person. This person has already become addicted to cheating and the rush it gives. This clearly needs to stop with some professional help. If you are into the habit of cheating, but you want to get out of it, then you will have to consult a counselor. Or you can get help from a professional marriage therapist.

4. Your significant other is always busy, and you are alone too much

Your partner is always active and busy with their work and activities. Whenever you need them, they cannot be there for you. There are times when the spouse is gone for months for work or anything else. They also have no time to take you out for lunch or some café to have good times together. In addition, whenever you are together, your partner is still on his or her phone, talking to a business associate or a co-worker. Even when you are together, they have no time for you. Their attention is always on something else. Because of this, you end up starting another affair with someone else just to fill the void. Despite the many reasons for cheating, it is never justified.

5. You simply feel dissatisfied with your married life

You are out on a business trip, and you call your partner to check up on them. However, when they received the call, there is a loud noise in the background, and they are in a hurry to speak with you. You feel neglected and as if you are unimportant to your partner. You simply feel dissatisfied that you go looking for another person whom you can connect with on an emotional level and, more importantly, physical level. Then you just created an affair outside your marriage.

None of these opinions can be dramatic, and these things can happen daily. Cheating does not start from the dirty texts but on a normal sunny day with a lot of opportunities to do so.

Understanding How Affairs End

When you start to see a therapist, you put things into perspective. You realize the different aspects of the marriage and the affair that challenged your union.

You can also attend group meetings, so you will have the advantage of meeting different people with different opinions, characters, strengths, and stories of how they are coping with infidelity. You will meet people whose partners have refused to have sex with them for so long, and this has made them miserable, thinking they cannot cheat on their spouse. And yet it is their partner who cheated on them, which was the reason for the absence of sex in the marriage in the first place. There are also other people who had issues in their relationships and found it hard to reconcile their differences, so they walked out. You will meet other people and hear their stories, and this will help you put your own story into perspective. Everyone experienced pain and suffering, and you are all trying to get past it.

Infidelity will bring so many complications and issues to the people involved; thus, this should be reduced when you are planning to separate. Affairs do not happen on their own, and this also applies to the procedure of healing after being betrayed. You have to look inward and reflect on how you can get past such an ordeal and not derail you from your path but put you on track toward healing and moving on.

If you are serious about making things work in your relationship, even after the infidelity episode in your lives, then you should confront the affair with some guidance from a professional. Doing so will help you and your partner overcome such awkward moments and help you both recover. You can use different evidence-based approaches when trying to solve infidelity, but most of the time, they cause trauma to the betrayed partner. A study has shown that when such secrets are revealed, both partners will experience mental depression and anxiety, and, at times, there will be suicidal thoughts. You can experience an increase in emotional and physical violence between the couple after the infidelity has been revealed.

In such a case, a couple should have a professional therapist to assist them regarding the issues of cheating in marriages. The therapist may not be there to heal the relationship exactly, but they will help you in coming into terms with the situation and deal with it with the best possible mindset. A lot of professionals feel that any problem related to infidelity should be solved or enhanced with therapy since dealing with infidelity is definitely difficult. You can choose to pursue other ways of being counseled after an affair. One method you can use to save your relationship is by addressing the impact of infidelity to the relationship, and then create a mutual understanding of the affair, talk about forgiveness and healing, and move on.

General therapy, most of the time, works for about two-thirds of the couples who have been through infidelity, according to a study. When a couple decides to stay together, both parties must try and identify areas that they should improve and commit themselves to. You should be able to rebuild trust once again in the relationship after it had been lost. If, statistically speaking, only 67 % of couples can move past the issue of infidelity, what happens to the other 33 %? In such a situation, it is highly likely that there will be hostility, conflict, and no concern for each other. Therefore, the couple usually breaks up. They end a relationship as a mutual decision or not. This is because relationships are meant to help us meet our desires, including love, affection, comfort, and security, among others. A relationship that does not meet such desires is prone to infidelity. Such a union has a problem and dysfunctionality that must be addressed through separation.

Have you ever thought of ending a relationship? This is very difficult, more so after being attached to the partner and developing feelings with a romantic partner. When a relationship ends, you will be in a situation where you experience separation distress. You will not only cry over the relationship, but you also despair, wondering if you can find someone new to share your life with and provide your need for love and affection. A stressful separation will depend on different people. Others may find it worth celebrating the end of a toxic relationship, but still, you can experience distress in other ways. Partners who arrive at a decision to end the relationship may still go through therapy in order to set their perspectives right. Talking to a therapist can help you open up and release your painful feelings.

How to Prevent Infidelity

You will be happier and more satisfied in life if you find someone you love, and at the same time, nothing will hurt you more than when the person you love is cheating on you. You may think that the stages of love, including falling in love and having a family, end with staying happily married after that. Things may be different in reality and more complex than this. In the case of infidelity, the following symptoms might show between the partners:

- Your relationship starts to be strained.
- The happiness and joy that you had with your partner fade away.
- You feel some distance from your partner.
- You start blaming yourself and think you are the problem.

- You start blaming your partner, claiming that they have changed.
- Hostility and anger will be the order of the day.
- You may have thoughts of making the wrong decisions and may want to leave.
- You will get drawn to other people.

When infidelity has been committed, some professionals find them in rebound relationships after a breakup, and it is normal but not recommended. Infidelity can be sorted out, and there are ways to help you stop it. Any person who is cheating will always say that the affair they had is over. This makes recovery from infidelity seem impossible. Many people who survive infidelity might face another hurdle in their relationships, as many couples still get affected by the affair that was over. You are not supposed to cheat when you are in a committed relationship, after all. The damage done might create a strain on your relationship; sometimes, the damage becomes irreparable. Therefore, there is a need to strategize ways on how to stop cheating, and having strong willpower is one of them.

Infidelity is much more complicated than simply cheating; only weak people stray, they say. There are so many reasons that a partner cheats, and they do so for complicated reasons, but sometimes, a cheating partner simply could not provide a valid reason that will satisfy their significant other. For that reason, you are advised not to focus on why your partner betrayed you, but how to prevent infidelity.

1. Avoid hanging out with someone of the opposite sex

When you go out with someone of the opposite sex who is not your partner, then you can easily get attracted sexually; thus, this is not advisable. For instance, you are not supposed to visit a co-worker in her or his hotel room.

2. Do not drink alcohol with the opposite sex

Alcohol will lower your inhibition, and most of us are aware of this. When you are under the influence of alcohol or a similar substance, then you are probably going to do some things that are out of character. According to studies, many occurrences of cheating were a result of taking alcohol or drugs.

3. Support your relationship

If you are in a functional relationship, and you cheated, you will feel guilty. And this will make you care for your partner more to compensate your bad deed. Do not let it come to this point. Here are some rules that will help you support your marriage:

- Always be kind to your partner.
- Do not feel any anger toward your spouse.
- Have an exclusive character.
- Accept your partner.
- Honor your partner.
- Have a private life with your spouse.

- Be loyal to your relationship.
- Love your partner.

These rules will assist you in improving your relationship with your partner, thus reducing any chances of betrayal.

4. Weigh the consequences of infidelity

The lies coming from a cheating wife, husband, or partner are compounded each time they meet with the third party. The act of lying becomes a tool to carry out their infidelity. The common thinking is, "I will not be caught." With such excuses, many people think they will not be caught, and they will not pay for their infidelity. But you know what they say; there is no secret that never comes out. Do not think that you will be safe and that you will not get caught. Most people who cheat are caught. If you get lucky not to get caught, then you will have the guilt inside you, tormenting you about the betrayal against your partner. The guilt alone will cause issues in your relationship. Cheating partners invest their time and attention on other things, thus bringing negative energies to the relationship. Infidelity is never a harmless activity. Cheating on the marriage will bring some emotional damage to your partner and may even frustrate your children if you have any.

5. Maintain moral codes

It does not matter whether it is a religious or a humanistic code; you have to do what is right, not only for you but also for your family. You have to set rules against infidelity and maintain them. Some cultures glorify infidelity, but morality and infidelity are things that depend on an individual's belief. In modern-day culture, never assume that your spouse can engage in infidelity. Work smart to make your relationship healthy, and never take anything for granted in your relationship.

Infidelity can take away everything that you treasure, and this will be evident around you. You can end an affair, and you will recover from this, but infidelity leaves scars and challenges for both the partners.

Chapter 3:

Overcoming Betrayal in a Relationship

Betrayal is one of the most devastating experiences an individual can go through in a relationship. For a person to be betrayed, they must put some trust in their spouse first. It is usually fairly impossible for someone to be betrayed if they did not trust the person they are in a relationship with. Therefore, by definition, betrayal entails the act of an individual violating your belief, as well as trust in them. The betrayal we shall discuss in this chapter refers to various elements and forms of betrayal appended to a relationship. For instance, a child may be betrayed by parents who fail to support or love him or her. A spouse, on the other side, may feel betrayed when a partner has an affair. Betrayal also includes a situation where your partner abuses or hurts you. This can happen when they put their interests first.

As pointed out earlier, betrayal is one of the losses a person can experience in a relationship. It is not only devastating but also downgrading in different ways. For instance, a partner in a relationship who has been betrayed will lose their self-esteem. Notice that we are referring to betrayal as a form of loss, meaning that it is descriptive of a person's consequences of betrayal. In society today, we still have trouble comprehending the concept of grief, as well as loss. We have a clear understanding of death; when an individual dies, we experience loss. However, all too often, we fail to recognize betrayal in relationships.

Betrayal in Relationships

Of course, there are different forms of relationship transgressions. They also vary in severity. With that said, when we mention different forms of transgressions, we also refer to issues, such as forgetting to pick up groceries from the store or the inability to tend to the needs of the kids. However, the most common form of betrayal in relationships is infidelity. Many couples may manage to overcome this form of betrayal, thereby allowing them to grow stronger. Others become more affected by the actions of their better half. How do they manage to overcome such situations in their lives? How do they manage to fit in once more? Research shows that there are two related concepts to this question. There is the relational commitment, as well as the capacity to forgive. In the same research conducted by Wohl and Ysseldyke in 2017, two studies indicated that there was a close relationship between commitment, as well as transgression. In one of the articles published by these authors, it was discussed that they established the severity of a person's transgressions to be appended to decreased commitment. In that case, the relationship was still mediated by forgiveness. The more a spouse is ready to forgive, the lesser the loss of commitment. They established that unforgiveness often causes a major decline in many relationships. As such, forgiveness assists a spouse to preserve pre-offense devotion, especially when relationships suffer a certain form of transgression. It is of significance to note that while research did not demonstrate the actual forgiveness and how it increases relational commitment following the transgression, it ends up mitigating the damage. This is followed by slowing down the decline in commitment.

What Happens When a Spouse Is Betrayed?

In a research study conducted by Finkel in 2002, it was concluded that there is a positive association or correlation between relational commitment, as well as forgiveness. Apparently, the results indicated that commitment usually inhibits destructive reactions to various forms of betrayal, including neglect. Some partners may choose to leave the relationship. On the other hand, other partners can resort to having low commitment levels that have no inhibitory effects. Such partners may easily acknowledge the value and importance of this research finding based on past experiences that involve destructive behaviors that may harm relationships. Now that we've highlighted the key areas of betrayal in relationships, it is important to comprehend the actual actions that a partner may take immediately after they discover that they have been betrayed.

What Can Happen After the Discovery of Betrayal?

One of the most damaging aspects of betrayal is the fact that a person's reality is undermined. This implies that the trust they once felt might suddenly crumble at some point. Their innocence is shattered abruptly. The victim is left wondering what really happened. How could that have happened to them? Who is the actual person who betrayed them? Some of these betrayals leave people with moving on as the only option. This is usually a choice as a form of healing. A person who has been betrayed feels abandoned.

- **Affairs are more complicated**

  In every relationship that has experienced some form of betrayal, affairs happen to be more complex.

The first question a person will ask themselves is if they should uphold their dignity and put an end to the abusive relationship. Another question they would ask is if they shall be able to maintain their dignity when trying to heal. Also, someone will be wondering if they can rebuild their trust. With that said, a serious betrayer will put their spouse in a difficult situation where they need to discern what could be best for them.

- **The victim may develop bouts of doubts—Could love still be alive?**

  In many cases of betrayal in a relationship, the person who has been betrayed will constantly wonder if love is still in existence.

The individual may even wonder if it would be wise to risk giving the partner another shot or if it would be a foolish mistake to trust them once more. Instead of acting impulsively, it may also be important to serve oneself by taking some time to sort out their feelings while finding some form of clarity regarding what may be best for themselves.

- **Denying the truth**

Living in denial is one of the most pronounced side effects of betrayal. Denial plays a major role in enhancing avoidance behavior, as well as addicted behavior. The person who has been abused, in turn, may abuse drugs or alcohol or indulge in emotional eating as a means of evading the situation.

They may also write their partner, who betrayed them, out of their lives. These are some of the feelings an individual harbor when they have been betrayed.

- **Repeated expressions of sorrow**

When the victim discovers that they have been betrayed by their partner, they may take some time to express sorrow, coupled with regret, repeatedly. Usually, in this phase, the betrayer is attempting to offer hope for healing. The two may even attempt to sign up for couple's therapy with the hope of finding some form of healing. It may be a move toward finding a safe haven filled with a peaceful environment where they can interact and hear each other. At this point, they may also uncover their feelings, as well as longstanding issues that could have created some environment engulfed with betrayal. Maybe with the support of a therapist, they could find a viable solution. All too often, the person who has been betrayed may take a risk by deciding to reveal their vulnerable feelings, which lie beneath their outrage.

- **The betrayed individual may experience loss**

  With betrayal, the victim may experience a loss that can affect them deeply. In that case, the person who has been betrayed will be grieving. Whether the aftermath will be expressed using apologies or by being ignored, it is still going to hurt. However, a person can heal. But usually, it may take longer to find peace.

- **The individual can harbor feelings of anger**

We all know that anger is not a good emotion. However, in a case where someone has been betrayed by their spouse, it becomes imperative to comprehend that there is a root cause of the feelings of anger. With that said, the main irony of betrayal is usually that when an individual is emotionally betrayed, they end up betraying themselves. How you may ask? Anger will make them feel as if they are exuding strength. However, in real sense, it only shows how much a person still cares. As reiterated by Janis Abrahams, if you constantly feel indignant, you can try to risk and show your soft side by expressing your anger, as well as initial outrage. In other situations, we may not have chipped into the contribution of betrayal. But, because we've been betrayed at some point in life, we may have to display our emotions and anger.

- ## The victim may forgive but not forget

According to one prominent poet known as William Blake, it is pretty easier to forgive your enemy than a friend. When an individual care about someone, it becomes difficult to believe that they can betray you in any way, especially when it first occurs to you. It even becomes more complicated when you realize that you cannot reverse their actions and your feelings. It becomes an internal conflict. In other cases, when someone is reeling from a loss that is pretty much devastating, it becomes easy to succumb to the role of the victim. Here, the person can refuse to go through an exploration of what actually happened in order to encourage that form of betrayal. It takes courage for a person to determine their input in the case of betrayal.

How to Overcome Betrayal

We have learned that nothing is as painful as experiencing betrayal in a relationship. In the process of accepting the fact that you have been betrayed, a person becomes unforgiving in many ways. When the betrayal occurs, it may appear as if everything is crashing down and coming to a stop. The pain of being betrayed touches the core of one's trust, as well as the soul. Therefore, it is going to be challenging for the victim to move on easily. Here are a few strategies that one can use to overcome betrayal.

- **Begin by honoring your emotions**

   Now that you are aware you've been betrayed, the first step toward sealing the issue is accepting that someone you loved, or still love, has betrayed you. Honor your emotions. Is it anger, mistrust, or fear, or loneliness? These emotions are authentic. Therefore, you need time to internalize the process of honoring and expressing them. You also need to pause often and take note of what has been felt emotionally.

- ## Take some time to yourself

  It is pretty difficult to handle the entire cycle of betrayal and still remain sane. While this is factual, you can try to spend some time alone, meditating, and thinking about how you can move on without harboring painful feelings that may cause you to retaliate. If a partner betrayed you, for instance, ask the person to give you some space during which you will be soul searching in order to determine what may have occurred. You may also want to go away and take some time off your reality.

- ## Try not to retaliate

  Because you have been betrayed, you will constantly feel the need to retaliate. In this phase, you will be putting yourself in danger by physically harming yourself. You may even harm others in the process. If you get to such a point, you should resort to seeking immediate professional assistance. This is because there is no positive vengeance, especially in the heat of such a moment. Of course, there will be possible lapses coupled with mindful awareness, which should not excuse the person who betrayed you in any way. Maybe they could not easily find the courage to actually face conflict in any way by expressing them. For that reason, you need to try not to retaliate because you may have played a role in enhancing your betrayal.

- **Speak with a shrink or a friend you trust**

  When betrayed, you should find a friend to discuss it with. This should be someone you trust. This is because the discussion will be a viable communication channel for healing. A therapist can also assist you in clearing your head and making a decision regarding the right steps to take. On the same note, you should also remember that one instance of betrayal should not make you distrust anyone.

- **You may choose to forgive**

  Forgiveness does not imply that you are condoning the act. It is a way toward moving on from resentment. By choosing to forgive, you will be paving a new path for your life. Forgiveness may also lead to compassion and, eventually, empathy.

How to Treat the Wound of Treason

In the wake of the discovery of cheating, you are likely to come across a variety of thoughts and feelings that will range from being numb to feeling that you are out of control and crazy. This can be brought about by post-infidelity stress. They are usually normal reactions in an abnormal situation, and you can be assisted in going through them. You can have a closer look at the causes, symptoms, and the treatment of post-infidelity stress. Post-infidelity stress cannot be an actual diagnosis to recover from an affair. The threats of a relationship cannot bring any danger to someone's life. There can be an attack and threat against emotional well-being that can lead to a reduction of psychological safety. Reactions can be a result that one realizes they can feel overwhelmed and stuck with no guidance on how to go ahead.

This can bring further issues to yourself and others, as well as your relationship, in case you wanted to reconcile. There are so many symptoms of intrusion that involve flashbacks, having nightmares, and being obsessed. This can be due to images that are associated with betrayal. Issues that you did not encounter before the affair took place will now be the source of pain. You will be so much tensed; you might not even recognize yourself. You might feel as if you will go crazy. Betrayed spouses will find themselves obsessed with each detail and will try to fix everything to find the truth. You can be out of control, and you will feel like you can't stop or move away from the overwhelming thoughts and perceptions. But of course, there are ways to get passed this.

Have a Normal Experience

You should always keep in mind that the vital thing about obsessive thinking is to have a typical response to trauma. When you are going through reality, you will be having disturbing and obsessive thoughts. For instance, your previous challenges will hold your assumptions and assimilate them with the truth.

Journal-keeping

If there is a solution to having obsessive thoughts, then it is journaling and writing down your thoughts. It can sound simple and unimportant, but noting down your thoughts will give you a platform to be uncensored with your thoughts and feelings. This will allow you to explore yourself, thus allowing you to have new insights and interpretations of the events that took place. You can be guided in tracking your progress, even your unanswered questions regarding the betrayal. You will gain clarity of thoughts by being aware of your emotions. You will be significantly prepared to deal with a high emotional state when you are interacting with your partner because you have already examined them through your journal.

Plan Your Worry Times

Put aside specific time daily and for a selected amount of time for being alone with your thoughts. It may seem weird, but you should allow yourself some time to worry, obsess, and try to go back to the haunting images of betrayal. If you have thoughts coming to your mind during the day, console yourself that you are saving them for "worry time." This is to assist indiscreet thoughts from taking over the entire day. As time goes by, your worry time will decrease in length and intensity.

Change the Channel

Try to think of your mind as something that can be controlled using a remote. Whenever you have unwanted thoughts or images, you can change the channel to anything grateful. Or you can desire to display positive memories with someone, having hope for the future, and having different visions on something.

Predict and Prepare for Flashbacks

You should be able to recognize the triggers to unwanted flashbacks, so you can deal with them better. When healing, you should, by all means, involve the partner who betrayed you, validate your experiences along the way, and try to help in creating a new script for your relationship, moving forward.

Replace Unhelpful Thoughts with Helpful Ones

When you realize that you are reflecting or you have specific thoughts, then you have to ask yourself this question, how will this help me or the situation that I am in? The ideas will assist in keeping you stuck, and most of the time, you feel entitled to the sentiments that you are feeling, such as anger. You should also remind yourself of the role of negative thoughts in your possible actions. You should know your goal.

Personal Soothing Methods

Exercise, massage or spa, a healthy diet, muscle relaxation, curing illness, deep breathing, and prayer are some of the things that can help you deal with your issues. For example, you should not berate yourself for your flashbacks, but you can try to remind yourself that you are healing through these methods. Whenever you encounter flashbacks, encourage yourself to think that this will come to pass.

A Moment at a Time

This can be another cliché statement, but it will be important to remind yourself that this moment will not take place again, and it will come to pass. Do not feel so low and discouraged when the healing process is taking centuries or if you have a negative moment. Do not be stressed when things look okay for a month, and then you encounter a setback as if you are back to zero. Take every moment the way it comes, prepare well, and always keep in mind that you will do what you can do.

Having Suitable Support

Most of the time, the betrayed spouse will isolate and withdraw from other people due to different motives. This can be due to shame and fear of being triggered and being asked questions by other people. It could also be because of being disconnected from other people, as well as thoughts that no one would understand your situation. If your mission was to reconcile, then get help from people who can support the relationship. Unsupportive people can cause you more damage, not putting into consideration where you are with the healing process. Be on a positive side, where you will have positive support that can assist you in stepping out of the problems that surround you; this can help you to have a healthy life through the aid of positive practices. You can put into consideration a support group. Get books that are appropriately related to the topic and read them. Try to be involved in activities that you once enjoyed.

Counseling

You should put in your mind that you have to visit a professional counselor. When you visit them, it does not mean that there is something not right with you, or you are insane. Visiting a counselor will give you an unbiased person in your corner; this individual can assist you in navigating the curing process in a manner that will not involve so much pain. The curing process will always be painful, but when you have a counselor, they can assist you in getting to know some tools that will make the process easily manageable. If you are trying to reconcile, then counseling can be considered as an option and should not be disregarded.

Shame

There are two types of shame when it comes to the issue of infidelity. The first one is when the unfaithful partner will console themselves that it wasn't their fault. They try to say that if they could have given more to the relationship, then it would not have happened. The second one is when the betrayed partner considers what others think about them.

There are just some reasons for cheating; understanding these steps will help you to recover from an affair. The path to healing and recovering from infidelity can be strenuous and complicated, but still, you should know it is not hopeless. Never think you are alone, and you should not walk through it alone. Some types of pain are more profound than the ones brought by an affair. There are so many cases of infidelity that have been encountered by different people, but there is no single spouse that has been able to avoid the wounds. The path to recovering from infidelity is always very long, and this makes many people wonder if they will ever be normal again. For other people, the wounds never heal. They will always be angry and desperate.

When they try to think of hope, they get affected by the thought that the joy they once had was taken away. They see the future with a lot of consequences. They think that life after being betrayed is not worth living. A lot of people will talk about the pain of betrayal as one of the worst experienced. Most of them can't imagine having a free and joyful life again because, for them, the deception of their partner is like an injury that has crippled them for the rest of their lives. They can't help to live the changed part of their lives, and they find it very difficult to assume that they were once cheated on in the relationship. Consequences must be there, either severe or regular, because of the decisions. What they never understand is that the future has so much for them, but they cannot imagine it because of the current perspective that they have.

Self-monitoring

Self-monitoring is the process through which you observe your behavior and evaluate it regularly with a view of aligning it with pre-set goals. You can do self-monitoring consciously and deliberately. It can also be done subconsciously and automatically.

The benefits of self-monitoring are quite immense to those who continuously practice the habit. When you are always aware of your behavior, it equips you with the right tool to achieve the desired behavioral changes. There are many ways that you can employ to monitor yourself to change your behavior.

Strategies for Self-monitoring

It is quite common for people to wish to change some of their behaviors. However, you may encounter challenges in determining how to do this. Tracking the frequency of exhibiting the target behavior and what exactly triggers it can also be a problem.

There are established techniques you can employ to monitor your behavior. These self-monitoring techniques equip you to recognize and keep track of your habits from your behavior. These strategies, once you apply them, can help you control your behavior effectively. They can also significantly help you to learn, identify, and increase beneficial social behaviors.

These are types of behavior that are necessary if you want to move on from a relationship issue and live a happy and successful life.

Once you have identified these self-monitoring techniques, all you need to do is watch your behavior over a given period. The following are some of the important strategies that you can employ to monitor your behavior effectively.

1. Identify the target behavior

The first step for you to succeed in achieving the desired behavioral change through self-monitoring is to identify the desired behavior that you want to change. Is it how you treat your spouse? Is it your inability to cope with infidelity? It is advisable to monitor just one behavior over a specific time. You need to prioritize the types of behavior you want to track to avoid getting distracted. You can choose the most critical behavior first, and you can gradually move down the list, in the order of their importance.

2. Make detailed observations of the target behavior

You need to observe the quality of the target behavior, as well as the frequency by which it takes place. Observing the quality of behavior helps you to reflect on the experience you have regarding a specific behavior. This includes the feelings that are evoked by a particular behavior.

Observing your target behavior could mean measuring the frequency and the duration a specific behavior occurs over a specific period.

Making detailed observations of the target behavior is an essential step in achieving your desired behavioral change. For example, if your goal is to quit talking to women whom you find attractive, you may be thinking of simply avoiding situations where you might find yourself talking to women. But after monitoring your habit for a while, you might be shocked to learn that you practice this almost every time there is an opportunity to do so.

The behavioral quality in this scenario involves the reflections you do concerning how you respond to the desire to talk to women. Ask yourself how you react once the temptation hits you. Can you resist the craving by practicing self-control, or you give in immediately when the craving is too strong?

3. Use rewards

You need to include rewards into the plan that you are developing. Rewards will help reinforce the desired qualities of your target behavior. This means each time you observe yourself doing the desired behavior, you promptly reward yourself. You also need to make the reward proportional to the desired behavior. For example, you can reward yourself with a walk or a movie each time you do self-study for one hour. If you attain the desired grade in your exam, you can reward yourself with an outing.

4. Seek help from your trusted friend

You can get the help of a trusted friend or family in identifying your target behavior. You also need to come up with a plan on how you will record and deal with the behaviors you desire to change. Such people will also give you support and motivation to push you to achieve your goals. For example, if you are targeting a daily work out as a form of coping from divorce, your friend can join you for the exercises. This will not only motivate you to achieve your target but will also ensure that you are accountable to someone. It is wise to enlist the help of a friend who is trying to implement the same behavioral change, even if their motivation is different.

How to Monitor Your Target Behaviors Through Recording

• Use of prompts

You can ask for the help of others in recording your target behaviors on a daily basis. They can remind you that you displayed the target behavior at a particular time, so you can account for it. For example, your target behavior is to stop talking about your ex who cheated on you. Your friend can help remind you whenever you start talking about it, whether   absent-mindedly   or consciously.

- ## Create charts to help you track your behaviors

  You can also come up with appropriate charts displaying specific columns for the behavior, frequency, and time. You then need to fill in the columns at specific times of each day. Record the behavior, the frequency at which the behavior occurs, and the time they occur. Alternatively, you can install the charts in your portable devices, such as your smartphone or laptop.

- ## Use a tape recorder

  If it proves to be impossible to monitor your behavior using a chart, then consider using a tape recorder.

You need to record yourself with an audio recorder or a video recorder. You can create time later to analyze your recordings. Count the number of times you exhibited a particular behavior and record the details on the charts.

- ## Use apps

If you own a smartphone, you can install monitoring apps that record the essential details of your behavior. These apps have particular features for recording specific details of the behavior. For example, you have included walking exercises as a way to heal. An app can be used to tell how far you have walked and the pace you held during your walk. Depending on your coping mechanisms, there might be apps for such, e.g., an app to track the calories your body has burn while you were exercising and an app that monitors your sleep habits as a way to address sleepless nights and anxiety.

- **Make a graph of the results**

  Once you have worked out the number of times you displayed a particular behavior, you can then present the data in a graph. This will ease the analysis and interpretation of the information. For example, you can easily interpret the frequency of a specific behavior from the data presented in a graph. It will also help you to compare the frequency of target behavior against the given time. This is an essential tool used to monitor your progress toward achieving the desired goal.

Making Use of the Results

1. Study the graph

The graph displaying your results will help you to know the frequency of occurrence of a behavior. It will also help you to establish the trend of a particular behavior over time.

The graph is also helpful in comparison of variables and in an analysis of the problem behaviors or the desired behaviors that you display often. Knowing this will help you to adjust your rewards and prompts to maximize the desired results. For example, if you intend to work out more often, then you can analyze the graph to know how many times you visit the gym. If you notice you frequently miss your gym appointments on a specific day, then you can analyze the routine of that particular day in order to fix it.

2. Start fading the prompts and rewards slowly

Once you notice an increase in your desirable behaviors, you should then reduce the use of your recording prompts and rewards. Start by using just half of the prompts, and eventually, you stop the use of the prompts completely. You can repeat the same process with your rewards.

3. Model your future efforts using the results

The moment you successfully create an effective routine to monitor and change your behavior, you can then use the same method to monitor and adjust your other undesirable behaviors. However, you should note each behavior is unique and, thus, may require that you carry out some slight adjustments in the routine you are using.

Benefits of Self-monitoring

- Self-monitoring can help you to build a solid structure that can help you monitor your progress in achieving your set goals. It allows you to make visible observations of your behavior through the use of external measures.

- Secondly, when you record your behavior, you change the occurrence of that behavior by being aware of it. Studies have shown the people who track the number of cigars they smoke each day tend to decrease the total number of cigarettes they smoke within a specific time.

- Moreover, self-monitoring helps in forming active programs that help change behaviors in the desired direction. This is because your measured progress leads to rewards or punishment.

- Self-monitoring also increases your awareness, as well as your consciousness and curiosity. Being aware of your behavior often prompts you to take responsibility for the consequences of the action rather than perpetually blaming other factors, such as your cheating husband or substance abuse.

- Self-monitoring can also be used to identify undesirable behaviors that you need to change. You are also empowered to take the initiative of changing such behaviors, thus enabling you to be accountable for them.

- Self-monitoring also comes with the beneficial interpersonal competition when you strive to break your previous records as you aim to achieve your goals.

Chapter 4:

Managing Resentment and Restoring Trust

Cheating in a relationship can cause some serious effects, such as damage to the self-esteem of the person cheated, loss of trust in the cheating partner, and emotional instability, among many others.

If the goal is to save the relationship, couples can overcome this challenge of infidelity. One of the ways of overcoming infidelity is managing resentment and restoring trust. Therefore, we are going to explore some of the ways through which one can avoid resenting the cheating partner and restore trust after the infidelity.

Forgiveness and Its Benefits

Learning to forgive can reduce the feelings of hurt and depression. Forgiveness can also increase compassion and helps to improve the physical symptoms that are related to harboring resentment and anger, such as headaches, back pain, stomachaches, and muscle tension. By holding on to anger and resentment, you are not doing your body and mind any justice. Consider the benefits of having plenty of physical energy and the importance of moving past hurtful experiences. Thinking of all the benefits, one can gain from letting go of resentment and, instead, work on healing negative emotions.

People equate forgiveness with being weak, and it is also largely believed that forgiving your partner for having an affair is like condoning or excusing the behavior. However, being a forgiving person is a form of strength, as it shows that you have no ill intentions toward your partner. Forgiving is a way of letting go so that you can begin the process of healing and moving on with your life. Forgiving is about giving yourself, your partner, and your children, if any, the kind of future that you wish and deserve to have. And this future should be unhindered by feelings of anger and resentment. It is about choosing to live a life where you do not allow others to have power over you by letting unresolved resentment and bitterness dominate you.

By practicing forgiveness, it turns the tables from feeling like a victim and becoming more of an empowered person. It is a general belief that forgiveness can allow one to break the cycle of pain and negativity and move on to a healthier life. You should remember that forgiveness has a lot to do with letting go of things that you have little control over. However, it takes time.

Personal Goals

Take a Look at the Circumstances

It is important to honestly reflect on the situations surrounding your partner's decision to have an affair with another person. If you try to see the situation objectively and you consider your responsibilities in the relationship, you may come to realize that your partner's decision to commit infidelity may have a direct link to the difficulties in the relationship. It is not to say that it warrants such behaviors or that it is okay or acceptable. Looking back at the situation where infidelity stemmed from will help you and your partner move past the blame game, which could be the only thing keeping you from forgiving your partner.

One such circumstance is sex or lack of it. A difference in sex drive is one of the major causes of infidelity in many relationships and marriages. It is even more prevalent when an individual in a relationship, rather than mutual consent, decides that sex is not very important and that it is unwanted. It creates a situation where one person in a relationship is contented to carry on without sex, while the other person is left to abstain against their wishes. It is like telling someone that you do not want sex anymore, and therefore, they should not, too. It is unfair and very inconsiderate of the partner.

Many people in this kind of situation opt to cheat, and some decide to leave the relationship. With some dose of compassion, it is understandable that one would feel the need to cheat, even if it is not socially and morally right to do so.

"Justified" is a very cruel word when talking about a hurtful act, such as infidelity. Cheating can never be justified. However, it can be understood if a spouse has not been available for a long period. It is best to address this by discussing this form of neglect with your partner. Sometimes, it can be because of your partner's illness, and hence, they cannot be available to you as they are incapacitated.

Therefore, if one tries to sincerely consider these situations, which led the partner to cheat, the partner who was betrayed may have a compassionate feeling and understanding as to why it happened. This way, one forgives the other and heals from the painful experience, and, in the process, the couple avoids resentment in the future.

Find the Lessons

Past experiences are the things that have shaped our lives and made us who we are today. Once you focus on the lessons learned from your past experiences, you will stop drowning in resentment. You need to realize that your partner's behaviors may have nothing to do with you, and it is not your fault. With all the attention and love, your partner may still end up cheating, as it is his or her choice.

For you to have a healthy relationship, it is important to let go of bad memories and start focusing on having a happy life. You deserve to be happy, just as much as everybody else. Holding onto resentment and bitterness is not worth sacrificing your joy. Take the experience as a priceless lesson and decide not to let what another person did to you consume you and dictate your feelings. All the pain, tears, and heartache can turn you into a resilient person, depending on how you react to the betrayal.

When we decide to let go and forgive our spouses despite his or her actions, it brings peace. Once you get rid of the anger, it no longer has control over you, and it releases you from the bondage of the wounds of your past. It is very important to understand about forgiveness that it is not only for the other person but also to heal ourselves. When you forgive, you take away the powers they had over your emotions. You may not have control over your past experiences, but you have full control of how you react and what you do in the present. When you get over the bitterness, animosity, and resentment, you experience freedom from the hurt and pain that once held you captive.

Transform From Being a Victim to a Victor

The moment you decide to look at your relationship with honesty—accepting both your mistakes and your partner's—you transition to feeling like a victor from being a victim. Your partner cheated on you, and that is the choice he or she made over the relationship and which you have no control over. Since you have no control over it, it is only logical that you try to accept it and move on. It is also where you retain power and control by not allowing your resentment and anger to take control of your life.

It is not to say you will never experience bitterness and anger of the past hurts and the lies that surround your spouse's cheating, but you can, however, control how you manage your anger instead of holding on to the angry feelings and replaying images in your memory that keeps you angry. You can redirect negative feelings and thoughts and focus on something more constructive.

Negative thoughts will drain your energy and hold you as a hostage of the past bad experiences, as they keep you from being in the present. But the good news is that there are ways or things we can do to overcome these negative thoughts. For example, you can meditate or do yoga. You can also surround yourself with positive-minded people, smile even if you do not feel like it, sing, list things that you are grateful for at the moment, and help someone else. Helping another person, in whatever way, will help shift your focus away from the pain that you are going through.

Confront Infidelity Wisely

The feeling of anger toward the guilty party is unquestionably warranted. After all, a huge relational injustice has occurred, and the affected partner venting just how disappointed and infuriated they are reasonable. However, if the relationship or marriage has to survive the affair, both parties have to get beyond the cheating and rebuild their relationship, and this means that the berating from the offended partner has to subside.

Having been discovered, the cheating partner may feel motivated to offer you support and compassion for what they put you through. If you continually and punitively shame their action, humiliate, and demean them, it can seriously damage their ego. This might only make things worse. They might find themselves lacking emotional support because of your unmitigated attacks.

Sometimes, having the courage to share what is beneath the anger, for example, is priceless. Explaining how devastating the affair has been for you, how you are heartbroken and hurt, and not knowing how to overcome it allows you to unload the baggage and start your journey to healing. Such words are a genuine admission of sorrow and vulnerability, and they are not about furiously criticizing the offender but giving them feedback as to how harmful their behavior had been to you. Such an assertive admission is more likely to draw the guilty party to confront their betrayal and begin showing empathy and compassion directly.

Take Full Responsibility for What Happened

If you are the cheating partner, begin by owning up to what you have done. It will not be helpful to try to fudge the truth, lie, or justify what happened. Explain to your partner about what happened clearly, and acknowledge that you made a terrible mistake and that you are responsible for the choices you made. Do not try to put what happened on your spouse and anyone outside the relationship, such as the other person in the affair. It is possible to feel like you had good reasons to have an affair, but it is helpful to realize that you have control over the choices you decide to take.

Decide to Trust Your Spouse Again

Rebuilding trust in a marriage after a case of infidelity does not happen overnight. It is a slow and progressive work that will take its time. Deciding to trust someone who betrayed you by having an affair with another person may sound impossible, but it is possible. And it is the best thing to do for your marriage if you are keen and determined to restore trust after infidelity.

When infidelity takes place, the partner who felt betrayed feels as if he or she could not trust again. However, with no trust between the partners, there is no relationship either. Therefore, if you decide to stay and rebuild the relationship, restoring trust after infidelity is the most important step of all.

So, to revive trust and rebuild your relationship, you have to come out of the loop of replaying the episodes of the affair in your thoughts. You need to break free and take small steps toward resurrecting your marriage after an affair.

Sever All Ties

Say you are the partner who was involved in the affair. You have to know that there is no chance of restoring trust if you try to maintain some form of communication with the person you had an affair with. You have to cut all ties to the relationship as soon as your spouse discovers the affair. You cut contact by not talking to them on the cell or via text. You quit interacting online, and most of all, you quit seeing them. That is if you intend to work on your relationship. The affair must completely come to an end if your goal is to restore trust in a damaged relationship. Let the other party know in crystal-clear terms that it is over, and inform your spouse that you have ended it or that you are planning to do so immediately.

The cheater needs to make sure that there is no further contact with the person they had an affair. Avoiding making contact, perhaps, is the most difficult thing to act on and implement. But for the sake of your marriage or relationship, you must do whatever you have to do to make it impossible for the two of you to communicate again. It could mean changing your cell phone number or the email address. It could also mean removing them from your social media, such as Facebook. An extreme situation is to skip town if it is necessary. You need to do this to ensure that there is no further contact, which can lead to more involvement.

Stay Present-Oriented

One difficult thing about restoring trust after being cheated on by your lover is staying in the present and focusing on the future, rather than living in the hurtful past. It is only natural to feel angry, hurt, and sad about the decisions your partner made, and you have every right to feel them all. However, eventually, you will have to let go of those feelings and focus only on the present and the days to come for a chance to re-establish trust. This course of action also allows you to work toward a more positive and open approach to the marriage. But if you can't let go of these feelings, it may be a sign that it is unworthy to stay in the relationship any further.

Trust Yourself

This is yet another important but difficult thing to achieve in a relationship after an affair. At this point, you might be starting to question your instincts. Maybe you think that you should have done some things differently or that you saw this coming. However, becoming aware of all the factors contributing to the partner's infidelity and moving forward are two important things in having a healthy relationship. It is important to understand that cheating is not an excuse to abuse your partner. Your spouse still deserves to be treated with respect.

Infidelity in marriage and relationships can cause some serious damage to people. Anger, bitterness, heartache, depression, and betrayal are feelings that can lead to resentment. However, if the goal is to salvage the relationship, your partner must learn how to manage these feelings and find ways that he or she can use them to restore and build trust in the relationship again.

Trust is not something that you earn; it is given. Any attempt to try and control your spouse, instead of trusting and respecting them to make their own decisions, will create unhealthy power dynamics in the relationship. It is not an easy job, working toward a healthy relationship, and trying to restore trust after cheating. It is a confusing experience, and I encourage you to try and use the above guidance to manage resentment while restoring trust in your relationship after infidelity.

Goals with Your Partner
Find a Relationship Therapist

Feeling anger and resentment is a natural response to the betrayal that you felt after your partner had an affair with someone else. Your partner broke your trust and the relationship, as well. Everything that happened comes with emotional reactions. The experience is very emotional and hurtful. Apologetic words may not help at this point because we need our partners to understand the pain that we are going through. Unless you feel your partner's empathy for what you are going through, nothing will change. Unless your spouse takes responsibility for cheating, the rest of the healing process, which includes grieving, reconnecting, and letting go, cannot take place.

Spouses who get betrayed by their partners and eventually forgive them may feel as if it is unfair that their partner "gets away" with cheating because they want to stay in the relationship. This creates anger and resentment that keeps you stuck in one place. No matter how much you got hurt, no one is actually getting away with it. Both of you have lost something after the affair. If you are suffering and your partner is aware that they are the cause of your pain, this awareness becomes the source of their pain, especially if they care about you.

Even though you are entitled to feel angry and hurt, this provides you an opportunity to reconnect with each other.

You cannot undo the past. You will only have to let go of the past if you honestly want to stay and rebuild the relationship together. You are going to focus more on the good and let the balance of nature outweigh the pain of cheating. This way, you are going to connect on a deeper level and recognize the fact that you are both suffering. It is alright to want some time to grieve the loss. It is also okay to seek help. Both of you can find a couple's counselor who can work with you, so you can reconnect and heal after an affair. You can build something new from there.

Progress, Not Perfection

It may take some time and practice for one to stop harboring difficult emotions, depending on the severity of anger and resentful feelings. You may not get rid of your resentment and anger completely, but instead of feeling pain in your belly when you think of your partner's betrayal, you may notice that you have progressed after experiencing only a short moment of frustrations and anger that quickly passes.

You might have been trying for months to redirect negative feelings and thoughts and shifting focus to more constructive tasks and ideas and come to realize that you still get angry. Do not be too hard on yourself; this normal because giving forgiveness may take long. You only need to be patient. However, if you feel like you need professional help to heal from anger and resentment, you can book an appointment with a mental health professional, and they can help you process your emotions and thoughts.

An unimaginable thing has happened; you just found out that your lover cheated on you. You now think that what you had is lost, and there is no way you are ever going to work things out again; break-up becomes the answer. On the contrary, for other people, they may still have feelings for their significant other, and given the circumstances, they may not want to let go and try to keep the relationship instead. However, it gets hard when they do not know how to restore and build trust after infidelity has taken place.

Rebuilding trust is possible. It requires a lot of work and commitment from both partners willing to heal the relationship. However, there is no guarantee that your partner will never stray again. You cannot control someone's decisions, and only he or she can make a choice. However, it is upon you to choose whether or not to trust your lover again.

Rigorous Honesty

The process of healing a relationship or marriage after infidelity starts and ends with the restoration of trust. So if cheaters want to salvage a damaged relationship, they must not just come clean about what has happened but also become rigorously honest about any other aspects of their life, both in the present and moving forward.

A cheater cannot automatically restore trust because the infidelity stopped. A person can restore trust through consistent accountability and telling the painful truth. Cheaters have to commit to living differently and sticking to certain boundaries. Most of all, a partner who cheated must be completely honest about everything all the time. They need to start telling the truth, with no fear, no matter what it is, even if they know it might upset their partner.

The cheating spouse must tell his or her significant other about everything, not just the things that are convenient to tell or something that they think will hurt less. With rigorous honesty, there are no more lies and secrets; he/she tells everything and keeps his or her partners in the loop about what they are doing or planning to do, for example, spending, gifts for the kids, trips to the gym sessions, problems at work, and any social interactions that their spouse might not agree with. They must learn how to be honest actively if they think there is something that his or her partner might need to know. They must volunteer and do it, even if it is something minor. The partner who was betrayed might get angry about the things that he or she will hear from you, but it will be worse if they found out about it on their own, especially if you did something to cover it up.

Communicate Openly

You may have known all about your partner, in and out, before the affair. Well, things have changed, and you are now dealing with the aftermath of the cheating. If you are the one who cheated, your spouse now sees you as a new person, so they may act differently from before. As a cheater, you need to find out what your spouse wants and focus on that. Also, you let your partner be aware of your needs. Both of you must be willing to respect the needs of each other, so you can move forward. Otherwise, it might be time to consider partying ways.

Do What Your Partner Ask From You

To restore trust after you cheated is very challenging because you are dealing with broken trust. For a person to restore trust after the occurrence of infidelity in a relationship or marriage, a spouse who cheated has to be ready and willing to do anything that their partner asks them to do, provided it is helpful to the relationship. It is true; you still have your own needs and rights, and this has to be within reason, but you need to realize that what cheating did was to create a reason for your partner to check on you and know your "secrets." For example, if your partner wants to check your calls, texts, emails, and social media accounts, you should be in a position to let him or her do so.

So, rebuilding trust after an affair calls for you to accept whatever your partner wants you to do for them. It is a way that will help them accept that you are not in that place anymore. It is something you should be willing to offer him or her, as it can restore trust and repair damage in a relationship.

See a Marriage Counselor

Affairs are painful experiences, and there is no doubt about that. It is a very emotional thing to go through, and it can be overwhelming sometimes. It will be a brilliant idea to seek help from a marriage counselor and sign up for infidelity counseling. A marriage counselor, using his or her expertise, will help to facilitate rebuilding trust after infidelity.

Given that they have skills on how to deal with all manner of marital issues and challenges, they will be in a good position to help you see the situation through in a way that facilitates the restoration of trust after cheating in a marriage. Also, they can provide you with a perspective that both partners may not have put into consideration.

Chapter 5:

When It Is Better to

Decide for Separation

Signs That Separation Is the Only Choice

Marital separation is not an easy matter to deal with. Separating with a spouse usually comes with a lot of negative impacts on you and your children. Before you finally decide to separate, ensure you have exhausted all the other available options to solve your differences. It is always good to examine your motives for separating before taking that step.

However, in some cases, marital separation is considered an excellent measure to heal a hurting marriage. In such cases, separation is not viewed as a negative step but as a valuable measure used to build an even better, stronger foundation for your marriage. Separation also offers an opportunity for hurting couples to avail of the marital triage. It is, therefore, essential for you to decide when to take the step of separating from your spouse. The following are some of the helpful signs that you can use to know when it is time to separate.

- **Your partner no longer participates in your marriage**

When your spouse fails to acknowledge that he or she still has a partner, then it is time to separate. You find that unlike before, your partner no longer has any time for you, or they are not as affectionate with you as they were before. Your partner may also fail to come home for days or weeks, and they do not provide any convincing reason for their absence. They may also retort to making their own travel plans without informing you. This could mean that you no longer exist in their world, thus the need to separate.

- **If you know that separation can improve the quality of your life, then do it**

If deep within yourself, you are convinced you will be better off without your partner, then it is time to separate. This usually happens after you have unsuccessfully tried to solve your issues. You may have explored all the available options at finding an amicable solution, and still, you find yourself back at the drawing board. You then feel you can't tolerate the problem anymore, and the only way to live a happy life is by separating with your spouse. At this point, if you can also sense your partner will also be relieved by your separation, then it is time for each of you to go your separate ways.

- **If the only reason you are still in marriage is finances**

You may justify staying in an unhappy marriage with financial excuses. You feel you will not manage to support yourself financially if you separate from your partner. However, this is the wrong reason that holds you back from a happy life. It is better to separate and live a modest life than to stay in a toxic environment. You should be ready to get multiple jobs to earn the income that you need to support yourself. You might also be forced to move to a smaller house and cut your luxurious lifestyle in order to save more. Separation comes with a lot of adjustments, which might be uncomfortable. However, it is better to embrace these adjustments than to spend the rest of your life with the wrong person.

- **If the kids are the only thing holding you back**

  Some people are afraid to move out of an unhappy relationship because they fear the negative impact that the separation might have on their kids. If the only reason you are still in that marriage is your kids, then you should know that staying in this toxic relationship is already subjecting them to untold suffering and unhappy life. Separation from your partner, who cheated on you, can have a positive impact on the kids, although they will be forced to cope with the stress that comes with separations. The positive outcome is that kids will get a chance to live a better life in a non-toxic environment, away from the drama.

- ## You are in a relationship with a narcissist

  If your cheating partner has been diagnosed as a narcissist, then it is time for you to separate from them. Narcissists are challenging to handle, and you may not want to spend the rest of your life with one. They can make your life a living hell. It is, however, unfortunate that narcissist tendencies seem to get worse with age, and as such, you may spend many years with one without knowing it. However, it is never too late to move out of a narcissistic relationship. When your partner steals money from you, cheats on you, and starts displaying all the narcissistic traits and tendencies, it is time for you to move on.

- ## Your partner is abusing you

  If your partner is abusive, it is time to consider separation. An abusive partner makes your home an unsafe environment for you and your kids. If you find yourself in such a situation, then it is advisable to take your children and look for a safer place to stay as soon as possible. Where domestic violence is involved, it is your responsibility to protect your children and yourself by moving out of your toxic home.

- ## Unrepentant partner

  Separation is also encouraged in cases where your spouse is adamant and has become apathetic or unrepentant; if they refuse to make amends on their unbecoming behavior, which causes stress to your relationship, then it is time to go. If you genuinely care about your marriage and you are doing everything to save it, then decide to separate for a while. This will give your partner a chance to introspect and make adjustments to their behavior.

However, you should first take time to search your own heart and objectively evaluate your actions and weaknesses.

- **You can't trust your partner again**

In cases where your partner cheated on you multiple times, it can completely erode your trust in them.

If they repented and tried to do everything to regain your confidence, but you still find it hard to trust them again, then separation may be the necessary step for you to take. Trust issues often impede a happy marriage, so if you have a healthy gut feeling that you will not be able to trust them again, then it is a sign that you should leave your partner. No marriage can work well without trust. Family experts hold that trust is the solid foundation from where a happy marriage is built.

- **If you are in love with someone else**
  You may have tried all you can to make up with your partner with no success, and you have now met

someone else whom you fell in love with. If this is the case, then it is time to separate with your partner in order to create space in your heart for the other person. You will get the necessary space to know if the feelings you have for this person are real or if it is just a result of the hurt and rejection from your unhappy marriage.

- ## **If counseling has failed**

  If you have been to counseling sessions with your spouse, which were not effective in solving your issues, then it is time to separate. The first step to solving marital problems is usually to have counseling sessions with your counselor, who will listen to both sides and advise you on the best way to find an amicable solution. However, if you have undergone many of these sessions, but you still face the same problems, then separation may be the next viable option. In some cases, it is your counselor who may suggest for you to separate.

- **You feel nothing about separating**

  You are ready for separation once you feel nothing about leaving your partner. In fact, whenever you envision your life without them, you feel just okay. Besides, if you have no feelings of loss or regrets leaving your partner, then this could be a good sign that, indeed, you are ready to separate.

Important Things to Do Before You Separate

Before you decide to move on with your life after an infidelity episode, consider the following steps.

- ## Consult your lawyer

   It is advisable to know what the law says about separation and how it applies to you. You need to make your decisions from a knowledgeable point rather than basing them on your emotions. For example, different states have different laws on divorce and separation. It is, therefore, essential to consult your lawyer to know what specific laws apply in your state.

- **Decide you want a separation**

    A separation is a life-changing event. You need to be very sure that you really want to separate. If you have doubts about taking the separation route, then maybe it is wise to give it some more thought. You need to acknowledge that separation will have an impact on you physically, financially, and emotionally.

- **Come up with a plan**

    Make a good plan on how you intend to carry on with your life once you are through with the separation process. Take note that your spousal support will not count once you separate. It is also essential to come up with a backup plan, just in case your spouse refuses to honor part of their separation agreements, for example, sharing custody of the child or if they refuse to move out of the house. It is also essential to involve your friends and family in all the plans you are making.

- **Make a realistic budget**

Your flow of income may change drastically once you separate. You, therefore, need to make some adjustments to your budget to reflect on these changes. Look keenly on your expenses and take appropriate budget cuts. Be realistic when coming up with your monthly needs to ensure you do not strain yourself financially.

• **Cancel your joint credit cards**

You need to cancel the joint credit card you own with your spouse once you decide to separate. This is important, especially if the cards have a balance that you do not want to assume responsibility for. You can also request your credit card provider to cancel any new charges. Alternatively, you can ask your spouse to be removed from the card if they are authorized users.

However, if you feel your joint credit cards may come handy in case of an emergency and you still want to keep it, then it is advisable to request a decrease in the limit.

- ## Close joint bank accounts

  It is also advisable to close any joint bank accounts you hold with your spouse once you make up your minds to separate. But if it is a must that you keep it open, ensure that you make arrangements with your bank to make it mandatory for both of your signatures to be availed before any transaction is undertaken. You should also request for the cancellation of any overdraft lines, as well as the equity lines. It is always the best idea to separate your finances as soon as possible.

- ## Set up an emergency fund

  You need to set aside some funds to get you going for a few months after the separation. This will give you enough room for adjustments as you settle down in your new place. You should also put aside some money to cover for your future emergency needs, such as paying for hospital bills, repaying overdue loans, or meeting your kid's future expenses.

- **Document all the financial information**

  After the separation, it may be a challenge for you to gain access to any financial information on your spouse's name. You need you to gather all the relevant financial information, such as their bills and account information. You also need to get copies of statements of accounts that go back at least five years. You should also make copies of all the important business and personal tax returns. Other relevant copies you should document include phone bills, debit card statements, and statements on debts you jointly own.

Steps to Take Once You Decide to Separate From Your Partner

Separating from your partner is never easy. You may undergo stressful moments during and after the separation process. Separation often involves a lot of legalities that may overwhelm you. You may find it a challenge knowing exactly what to do and how to do it. There are a number of steps that could much guide you through the rough period of marriage separation.

Step1: Accept Yourself and Your Decisions

Separation can be overwhelming. Separating from a partner whom you have known for a long time and whom you have spent both your best and worst moments of life is never easy. You may find yourself stuck in denial. However, it is crucial that you give yourself the necessary time to accept your situation and come into terms with what has happened in your marriage.

If possible, find a good support network comprising of understanding family and friends. You also need to freely share your feelings with the people close to you. When you talk out your feelings, you will get the much-needed help to fully accept what is taking place in your life.

Step 2: Consider the Legalities Involved

Your next step should be hiring a divorce lawyer to help you with the legalities involved in the separation process. Go for an attorney who is well-experienced in matters of divorce and separation. It is advisable to engage the services of a lawyer even if you are separating with your partner on amicable or friendly terms. Filing for separation may involve a lot of legal procedures that may present a challenge if you do it on your own. A trusted, affordable lawyer can make this process as smooth as possible for you.

Step 3: Decide Who Gets What

You need to come up with an amicable agreement with your partner on the sharing of assets and responsibilities once you make up your minds to separate. Deciding who gets what in terms of property and responsibilities, such as child custody, is crucial for a stress-free separation.

It is essential to involve your lawyers in these decisions. Let your attorney know how you intend to split your assets, as well as how you plan to share your children. When it comes to deciding on sharing your children, the court will always have a say. The court makes decisions based on the children's age and health. It will also consider your financial status and capability to offer adequate care for your kids. You need to agree with your partner to talk about these issues to come up with a mutual agreement in order to avoid long, stressful court processes.

Step 4: Disengage From Your Partner Emotionally

You then need to start disengaging from your partner physically and, most importantly, emotionally. This means you are disconnecting from some of the roles and expectations of your partner. You also need to stop any romantic involvements with your partner. Emotional disengagement may involve some mourning process. You mourn your past good thoughts and experiences you had with your partner.

This stage is usually the most challenging and highly emotional. However, it is the most crucial part of the separation process that will help you to move on smoothly with your life. Accepting that one chapter of your life is over and another more exciting one is about to start is very important.

Step 5: Embrace Your New Life

Embracing your new life means getting ready to live as a single but content person. You need to learn to live alone again, being free to do whatever you want or meeting whoever you want without feeling guilty. Start rebuilding your life again. Come up with a fresh vision for your life, and start rebuilding your dreams and aspirations. It is also essential to keep in mind that you do not need anyone's approval to lead an amazing life and achieve your life's dreams. Separation is not a death sentence, but it is an opportunity to reexamine your life and rebuild yourself in order to be happy again.

In case you meet a fantastic person who interests you, do not fear going out with them. Get to know them better. Identify their values and principles. Find out if there is anything common you share with them. However, you should be careful not to get involved too soon.

How to Overcome the Hurt That Comes With Separation as a Result of Infidelity

You have been a very loving, dedicate, and supportive partner, yet your spouse cheated on you. It is natural to be devastated and confused. The hurt that comes with the betrayal can be overwhelming. You feel like your whole world has shattered, and you are at a loss on what to do.

However, despite the hurt that comes with infidelity, you need to make a conscious effort to get past all the pain. You should, however, acknowledge it is not an easy task. Studies estimate that it takes up to two years to completely heal from the hurt that comes with infidelity. However, although the pain will not go away overnight, it will eventually end. You do not need to spend the entire to years living in misery. The following are some of the ways you can use to overcome the pain and stress that comes with infidelity:

- **Take time to mourn**

    You need to take a moment to grieve for the loss that comes with infidelity. There are five stages of grieving:

    - Denial
    - Anger
    - Bargaining
    - Acceptance

    You need to go through each stage conclusively in order to heal completely. The last stage is always crucial. Once you have accepted that your partner actually cheated on you, only then will you be able to get over your pain and misery.

- **Take good care of yourself**

  The stress and pain that comes with infidelity can be so overwhelming that you ignore taking good care of yourself. You need to eat well, have enough sleep, and engage in beneficial workouts to maintain good health.

  It also helps your mind to stay focused in order to make critical decisions concerning your future.

  When you eat healthy food and have enough sleep, then you will relax more, and your moods will improve significantly. Exercise also distracts you from those painful memories that come after infidelity.

- **Do the things you enjoy more**

  You need to spend more time doing the things you love. You can also take up new hobbies to distract you from your pain. Go out and get yourself a treat, such as watching a new movie or having your favorite cup of coffee. You can also take up a new class to keep you busy and focused on other things.

- **Get the details of the affair**

  For you to heal completely, understand how and why the affair happened. You may need to book counseling sessions with a marriage therapist to help you both go through this. During the counseling sessions, you should ask all the questions on your mind. Ensure you get all the answers to help you move on. It is also essential to be patient with your healing process. Healing usually takes time, but focus on overcoming the pain first.

- ## Do not blame yourself

  It can be so easy to start blaming yourself for your partner's cheating ways. You may think it was your fault that they cheated. But the truth is you had no role to play in their infidelity. The choice was theirs to make. There is simply no excuse for having an affair, even if one is unhappy in a relationship. A good relationship is set on the foundation of unconditional love, and each partner must learn to be patient, understanding, and compassionate with each other. Issues that are rocking the marriage must be dealt with head-on rather than resorting to the temporary comfort found in affairs.

- **Know it is reasonable to feel hurt**

  After you discover your partner's cheating, you may experience a myriad of conflicting emotions. At one point, you love them so much, and the next minute, you loathe them with all your heart. You may also experience significant feelings of embarrassment, guilt, hope, and love all mixed up. All these conflicting feelings are real and normal. However, you should know that all these will change with time. You need to give yourself more time to think clearly and to identify your true feelings toward your partner.

• **Talk to someone**

You need to find a good support
network made up of close friends
and family to talk to after the affair.
Do not keep the pain and hurt all to
yourself. You may think you have
the power to handle the problem on
your own. However, it is advisable to
seek help from those you trust the
most.

Alternatively, you can seek
counseling from a reliable therapist.
Ensure you state your problem
clearly and objectively. Whatever
you do, do not rely only on your
reasoning and inner voice. Your
brain can convince you that you are
the one to blame for the affair, that
you are not caring enough, or that
you are not that pretty. You then

start justifying your partner's infidelity.

- **Keep a journal**

  Whenever you write down how you feel at a particular moment, you help your mind to release some of the negative emotions trapped inside it. You need to practice keeping a journal, and this will help you to release some of the pain you are feeling. You need to get a pen and paper, or install a journal app on your phone and start writing down all your daily thoughts and feelings concerning the affair.

How to Move on After the Separation

Having a divorce or separating from a partner is never the end of the world. You can still move on and get a better partner or remain single to recollect yourself emotionally. Here are some of the ways to move on without further heartbreak.

- **Forgive yourself and your partner**

  Once you have separated with your partner, you may be tempted to think you did not make the right decision. You may also have bitter feelings toward your partner. You tend to think that if he had not cheated, you would not be going through the pain you are in. But it is good to remember that all human beings make mistakes, and it is essential to learn from those mistakes. Learn to forgive those who hurt you if you want to heal entirely and move on with your life once again.

- ## Forget all your regrets

  Once the relationship ends because of infidelity, you may dwell on how you should have done something differently, or you start regretting the wrong things you did that made your partner cheat on you. When you have regrets, you open the flood gates of self-inflicted suffering. You need to forget the past; what you did or failed to do is now in the past. Bing your mind to the present. Accept that the relationship has ended, and focus on building your future once again. Pick up the important lessons from your previous relationship, and get rid of all the other negative thoughts.

- **Do not be tempted to get back together**

  You may start longing for your ex, especially when you start focusing on their good side. You may, once in a while, imagine they were perfect while you were the one at fault. But the truth is that both of you have your unique strengths and weaknesses, and the strengths of the cheating partner are no reason for you to get back with them once again. You have to let go.

- **Do not regret the time you lost**

  You will be tempted to think of your past relationship as a lost and wasted time. You think of all the opportunities you missed while dating your former partner. Stop focusing on the past and all the great things you think you missed. Instead, focus on the lessons you learned from that relationship. Some of the other positive things to focus on include the friendships and the experiences you made.

When you focus on the positive things, you are most likely to move on faster. You become empowered rather than being the victim.

- **Connect with other people**

  After the end of your relationship, it is essential to get together with the people you share the same interest with. These could be the people who received less of your attention when you were dating. You need to spend time with people who make you happy, energetic, and passionate again. Such people will help you get over your loss quickly.

- ## **Focus on the next chapter**

   The end of your relationship is simply the transition into the next chapter of your life. Therefore, you need to stay positive and focus on your future relationship. Be excited at the prospect of meeting new people who will treat you much better than your former partner. Let go of the past and its pain, and focus on building a happier, brighter future. Besides, if you feel your last relationship was holding you from accomplishing some of your dreams and aspirations, then start focusing on achieving them once you are free from the past relationship.

Bonus Test: The Perfect Test to Find Out if Your Partner Is Cheating on You

Do you think your wife is betraying you? Does your boyfriend have a lover? Find out with this test. Answer all the following questions and discover the risk of betrayal of your love relationship:

1. Has your partner recently spent more time looking after his or her physical appearance?

   Yes (1 point)

   No (0 point)

   I do not pay any attention (0 point)

2. Has your partner been more tolerant of you lately?

   Yes (0.5 point)

   No (0 point)

3. Does your partner lock some of his/her drawers?

Yes (2 points)

No (0 point)

4. When the phone rings, does your partner leave the room to answer it?

Yes (1 point)

No (0 point)

5. Does your partner tell you lies?

Yes (2 points)

No (0 point)

Yes, so they will not be scolded (1 point)

6. How does your partner react to your proposals?

He or she often accepts or agrees (0 point)

He or she often uses fatigue as a reason to refuse (1 point)

He or she accepts but, a few times, without enthusiasm (0.5 point)

7. Your husband or wife went out, and if you asked where he or she went, he or she is vague about it.

It never happens (0 point)

Occasionally, but you do not investigate (0.5 point)

Lately, it happens more frequently (1 point)

8. Have you noticed that in the last few months, your boyfriend or girlfriend has changed the password of his or her computer or email, or a new email account has been created?

No, it did not happen (0 point)

I do not think so; maybe it was done for greater security (0 point)

Yes, it happened (1 point)

9. Has your partner recently changed his/her habits and schedules?

Yes (0.5 point)

No (0 point)

10. Does your husband or wife have mood swings, often changing from joy to sadness, and vice versa?

No, it does not happen (0 point)

It has always been like this (0 point)

Lately, he has mood swings (0.5 point)

11. Does your partner have a little desire to be with you?

He or she always has the same desire, more or less (0 point)

Lately, he or she has less desire (1 point)

If we can, we prefer to do things separately, each with spaces (0.5 point)

12.   If you wear a new dress, does your partner notice it?

Yes (0 point)

No (0.5 point)

13.   Has your partner known and met new people?

Yes (0.5 point)

No (0 point)

14.   Does your husband or wife emphasize—with jokes and gestures—your routine?

Yes (1 point)

No (0 point)

15.   Does your partner tend to prefer group outings and feel bored when you are alone together?

Yes (1 point)

No (0 point)

16.   Has your partner recently enrolled in a class without asking to involve you, too?

Yes (1 point)

No (0 point)

17.   Has your husband or wife started going to the gym?

Yes (0.5 point)

No (0 point)

18.   Is your partner often on the phone, and he or she receives SMS messages at different times?

Yes (2 points) No (0 point)

Count the points for the answers you gave to find out if your partner is loyal to you.

From 0-9 points — Sure love, you are mutually faithful and satisfied with your relationship. If it was a fairy tale, the phrase could be used, and they lived happily ever after. Until you know how to draw stimuli from your relationship then you will be happy in love. But remember that eternal love lasts for 18 months, according to statistics! It is up to you to keep the relationship alive by listening to each other. And taking space and time for you. Maybe doing a nice vacation from time to time.

From 10-18 points — If you do not repair your damages. Routine increases the risk of infidelity. It is okay to be sure of yourself and of your relationship, but you risk to take your love for granted, and that is the first step to fall into routine and monotony, to encourage people to look for certain emotions elsewhere. Curiosity and passion must never be lacking, and out there is full of beautiful women or interesting men. Be careful.

Conclusion

Thank you for reading through the end of *Healing From Infidelity: A Survival Guide for Happy Couples. Let's Save a Contemporary Marriage From the Main Issue of Our Generation: The Divorce!* This book is a survival guide for those who have been part of relationships filled with toxic energy. You will learn that infidelity has shattered some of the strongest relationships in the world. It has also left behind negative feelings, including betrayal, anger, as well as guilt on innocent souls. For most married people who have been in such relationships but have breached their loyalty in one way or another, this is the perfect book for you to read.

The American Association for Marriage notes that it can be challenging to overcome those feelings. Therefore, an individual requires the support of a family, friends, or a professional therapist to cope with the situation. For some couples, an affair is a heavyweight to bear. In such cases, parting ways could be the only solution to the problem. However, before a fighting couple heads out the door, there are various steps that may be taken to help the relationship get right back on track. Experts suggest that there are different reasons that someone may decide to have an affair. In this manuscript, you will learn the definition of infidelity, including why someone in a serious relationship would opt to seek counseling instead of leaving their partner when they have been cheated.

If you have experienced any of this, perhaps, the next step is to start practicing what has been discussed in the book. What you need to ensure is that you understand the elements of infidelity to a great depth and incorporate the skills used in overcoming the challenges involved. Having understood that, it is also important to comprehend that sometimes, infidelity is all about a case of poor understanding of the situation that a couple is in.

Yes, an individual may feel unsatisfied in their marriage, and for that reason, they may get into a relationship with a co-worker after a few glasses of wine, which may easily lead to a lack of impulse control. Most commonly, infidelity is a result of a search for emotional connection. This implies that someone may be seeking attention from a different person other than their spouse. They may need a stranger to soothe their ego or flatter them. Whatever a person's reason for the affair is, the impact infidelity leaves on relationships is devastating.

Learning that your spouse has an affair is not only earth-shattering but also heartbreaking. When you get married, it is often natural to define yourself based on your marriage. For some reason, you may even lose yourself in the marriage. Therefore, it only makes sense that you become depressed when you have discovered your spouse is cheating and that you may lose your identity with it. You may even succumb to anxiety and other related mental illnesses. You should begin to question what is real, including what you want when it comes to intimacy.

In that regard, there is really no way to deal with a partner's disregard for marriage or relationship single-handedly. Some of the spouses who have been hurt choose to end their relationships based on how they feel. Others choose to create a new experience for themselves, straight from the ashes of the past relationship. None of these paths is easy to take. At the same time, it is not really easy to make that choice or decision. However, you will realize that it is important to choose a way forward when it comes to healing after betrayal. You shall also settle on some common ground with your spouse if you decide to stay in your relationship.

You learned from the chapters in this book that, whatever the main reason for the affair, infidelity ruins several relationships every now and then. Not only does it leave you questioning your sanity, but also everything else that you believed in your relationship.

Infidelity is crippling in many ways. But the most important thing is, after everything, you get back up and start over, whether with your partner or on your own.

NARCISSISTIC
ABUSE

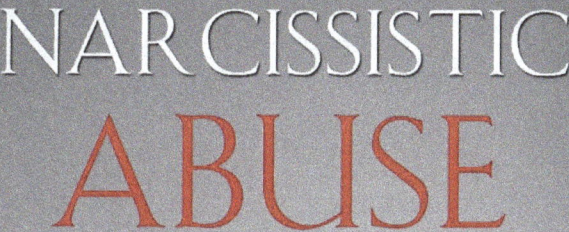

SECRETS AND ANSWERS ABOUT NARCISSISM TO FIND OUT THE
RECOVERY OF YOUR RELATIONSHIP. HELPFUL GUIDE TO BE
CODEPENDENT NO MORE

MELODY ROMIG

How to
HANDLE A
NARCISSIST

An ultimate guide to recovery from emotional and narcissistic abuse. Understanding and managing narcissism. How to become the narcissist's nightmare and kill a narcissist

MELODY ROMIG

CPSIA information can be obtained
at www.ICGtesting.com
Printed in the USA
BVHW051358080321
601998BV00011BA/1113